JOHN ROMERIL was born in Melbourne in 1945 and while a Monash University undergraduate wrote his first plays, the most noteworthy being *I Don't Know Who to Feel Sorry For* (1969) and *Chicago, Chicago* (1969–70). Romeril helped found the Australian Performing Group in 1970, and until it wound-up in 1981 the first performances of his plays were usually at the Pram Factory. Examples include *Mrs Thally F*, *Bastardy*, *The Floating World*, *The Golden Holden*, *Mickey's Moomba* and *Carboni*. He co-wrote APG successes like *Marvellous Melbourne*, *The Hills Family Show*, *Dudder*s and *Waltzing Matilda*; and collaborated on most of the APG's outdoor, factory and touring shows.

In 1974 Romeril wrote the screenplay for *The Great McCarthy*, and his occasional film and television writing includes a twelve-part series for the ABC's education unit, *Six of the Best* (1982); and, with Rachel Perkins, *One Night The Moon* (2000).

Romeril's produced plays, premiered by various managements during the 1980s include *Samizdat*, *Definitely the Last*, *Jonah*, *The Kelly Dance*, *Legends*, *Lost Weekend*, *Top End* and *Koori Radio*, and he helped shape Manning Clark's *History of Australia: The Musical*. Produced plays from the 1990s include: *Black Cargo*, *Bring Down the House*, *Reading Boy*, *Doing the Block*, *Expo: The Human Factor*, *Acronetic*, *Kate 'n' Shiner*, *Love Suicides* and *Hanoi-Melbourne*.

Romeril's most recent produced major play was for Playbox, *Miss Tanaka* (2001). Since then he has concentrated on dramaturgical work, often with young writers; on research-driven community projects such as *Landmines*, *The Dukes of Windsor* and *Dancing The Line*, which await production; and on his role as Honorary Chair of Strange Fruit (since 2006), a Melbourne-based largely outdoor physical performance group whose work on sway poles has toured the world.

He has been Playwright-in-Residence with certain theatre companies and tertiary institutions thanks to support from the Literature Board of the Australia Council, and educational, civic and sometimes philanthropic entities. Prizes include the Canada-Australia Literary Award (1976) and the Patrick White Award (2008).

While in a relationship with the painter Christine he was stepfather to Angus, Sibyll and Tessa; is godfather to Finn Robertson; and for 25 years has been the partner of producer-presenter Rosemary Hinde.

Love Suicides

John Romeril

CURRENCY PRESS
The performing arts publisher

First published in 1997
by Currency Press Pty Ltd,
Gadigal Land, Suite 310, 46-56 Kippax Street, Surry Hills NSW 2010 Australia
enquiries@currency.com.au
www.currency.com.au

In association with Playbox Theatre Centre.

Reprinted 2013.

NATIONAL LIBRARY OF AUSTRALIA CIP DATA
Romeril, John, 1945–.
    Love Suicides
    ISBN 9780868195155
    1. Australian, drama—20th century.
    I. Playbox Theatre (Melbourne, Vic.). II. Title.
    (Series: Current theatre series).
    A822.3
Typeset by Erin Dewar for Currency Press.
Cover design by Katy Wall for Currency Press.

Currency Press acknowledges the Traditional Owners of the Country on which we live and work. We pay our respects to all Aboriginal and Torres Strait Islander Elders, past and present.

Contents

Author's Note

Based on the double-suicide genre of plays pioneered and made famous by Chikamatsu Monzaemon, especially the example he set in 1703 with *Sonezaki Shinju*. I consider him the first great city playwright of our region. My play would probably not exist but for the active interest and encouragement of Peter J. Wilson, artistic director of Skylark, the Canberra-based puppetry company. I dedicate it to him, and to two other colleagues, the designer Richard Jeziorny and Noriko Nishimoto (of Spare Parts in Perth). This team of gifted people informed and supported the work over a long period. It was also underwritten by the Australia Council in the form of an Australian Artists' Creative Fellowship which freed me to deepen my grasp of the theatre in Japan. There is a fifth player, my partner Rosemary Hinde. Her dedication to the cause of Asia-Australia cultural relations has long been an inspiration to me, a lived example of how Australians in the arts can 'orient' their thinking.

John Romeril
September 1997

Love Suicides was first produced by the Playbox Theatre Centre and Company Skylark at the Street Theatre, Canberra, on 25 October 1997 with the following cast:

PARIS	*Simon Wilton*
OHATSU	*Asako Izawa*
MINH / NARRATOR	*Miki Oikawa*
GAVIN / FOX / PARIS PUPPET	*John Hunt*
KEIKO / DANCER	*Yumi Umiumare*
OHATSU PUPPET / ALBERT PUPPET	*Peter Wilson*
MUSICIANS	*Peter Neville, Angus Ibbot, Satsuki Odamura*

Director, Bruce Myles
Puppetry Director, Peter Wilson
Designer, Richard Jeziorny
Lighting Designer, Phil Lethlean
Composer / Musical Director, Peter Neville
Puppet Maker, Rob Matson

CHARACTERS

The performers comprise four actors, two puppeteers and three musicians.

The actors play the following roles:

MARK PARIS, a failed corporate whiz kid facing jail
OHATSU, from Osaka visiting Perth and soon to be married
KEIKO, a dead friend who functions as a ghost, primarily a dance role
MINH, a hotel staff member
NARRATOR
The actor who plays the role of Minh also plays the narrator.
Essentially, Keiko 'dances' the story and Minh 'tells' the story.

The puppeteers operate:

PUPPET PARIS, puppet version of Mark Paris
PUPPET OHATSU, puppet version of Ohatsu
ALBERT, a barman
OHATSU'S FAMILY and other puppet and scenic elements

One of the puppeteers also plays the roles of:

FOX, a company lawyer
GAVIN, a stalker-creditor
The actor who plays Ohatsu speaks the dialogue for the Puppet Ohatsu, as does the Paris actor for the Puppet Paris, unless otherwise indicated. A masked operator works each puppet.

The three musicians' principal instruments are piano, guitar, shamisen and koto. Two of the musicians also play the roles of:

MCSCRAG, a finance journalist
FINN, a real estate developer

SETTINGS

Act One is set in several locales in and around a Perth luxury hotel.

Act Two is the near-empty 'dream home' that belonged to Paris.

Act Three is set in King's Park, 1997.

A revolving mezzanine unit provides an upper playing level for all three acts. At this level, in Act One, the characters wait for the lift, and the unit supports the hotel wall. In Act Two the unit becomes a deck flanking the house, and it supports the swimming pool wall. As an open structure in Act Three it functions as an information/display area in King's Park. The space to either side is occupied by band members.

ACT ONE

EVENTS ABOVE EVENTS BELOW
EVENTS ABOVE AND BELOW

High above the stage, PARIS *is at work on a treadometer or similar piece of equipment in the gym of a luxury hotel. He has discarded his jacket and wears a t-shirt.*

On the stage floor level, in one of the band areas, KEIKO, MINH, OHATSU, *the* PUPPET OHATSU *(costumed identically to her namesake) and the koto player are seen. The image is little more than the faces of the five Japanese women.*

In the opening song, hand-held lighting, spotlights and downshafts of light give an overall impression that the cast and objects are 'hovering' in space.

PARIS *sings the first two lines of the song, then the women in the band area join in. They splay their fans, and the* PUPPET OHATSU *uses her fan to beat a drum.*

KEIKO *breaks from this line-up into a dance. Hers is a dance role and here she functions like a mistress of ceremonies, a shamanistic figure, 'dancing' up the locale and the characters, 'triggering' the story.*

When MINH *and the* PUPPET OHATSU *move off, ready to enter the story,* OHATSU *remains in her opening position, seemingly in the role of a singer and a part of the band.*

The opening song introduces 'theatrical' effects, plays with scale, and establishes the ways in which props, puppetry, etc, will be utilised. It allows us to sample different parts of the space, focusing first this character, now this.

SONG: You can kick / kick / kick-start a story,
         Get it off to a flying start.
         Add a fan fan fan / a fan-fare / beat a drum,
         A story can start in a thousand ways.

         You can raise / part / lower—a curtain,
         No-one's certain what's going on,
         Fire! a flare through smoke-filled air,
         A cannon sounds in the gloom,
         Blood is spurting people hurting,
         Or is it a loony tune?
         Show your teeth and grin,
         Tell a joke to warm the room,
         This is looking fun.

         There's a whistle a pistol a siren,
         The firing of a starter's gun,
         Ready steady you can go!
         Getaway out of the blocks,
         You can take your marks take your time or take away the
              chocks,
         Toss a coin and join a huddle in the middle,
         Making like a rugby scrum,
         Up goes the ball let a flag fall down come your tumbling
              stocks.

         You can draw a line in the sand—draw a heart on a wall,
         Draw a moral start a quarrel aim a barb,
         The players appear in curious garb,
         Entering one by one.
         But whatever's said whatever's done,
         Whatever's said whatever's done,
         Whatever's said whatever's done,
         The moment you start a story,
         After you start a story,
         Once a story's begun,
         You gotta letta,
         Gotta letta,
         Gotta let a story run!

A procession of shopping bags approaches, amongst them the PUPPET OHATSU *and* FOX, *sporting a fox-like half-mask. A vamp under.* MINH, *a uniformed Vietnamese hotel staff member, narrates. The* PUPPET OHATSU'*s dialogue is spoken by* OHATSU, *who remains in the band area, thus, in a way, representing a bunraku narrator, flanking the action and relating the story.*

MINH: A modern-day Japanese princess, is returning from a shopping expedition. She is an international guest at a five star hotel. Keeping her company is a company lawyer, a friend of her father's. He looks after her family's affairs here in Australia. She thinks of him as a fox—probably because he works for the firm of Briar Bramble Black Berry and Fox. This I don't know. I'm a mere employee at my station trying not to look like a cake decoration. May I take those for you? I can?

OHATSU: You may.

FOX: Here.

FOX *tips* MINH *for the service.*

MINH: Thank you.

FOX: Don't spend it all at once.

As the shopping parcels gather round MINH, *the song lyric resumes.*

SONG: It's a regular / Shangrila / with the / aura / of a / DREAM!
It's a synonym for heaven—the antonym of hell.
Check in—check out what we sell.
It's a twenty make that thirty sorry forty storey
Five-star Perth hotel.
Looking at the foyer,
If you're a foyer-voyeur,
We got a foyer for ya,
Well worth looking on.

MINH, FOX, *the* PUPPET OHATSU *and the shopping have moved away.* PARIS *sings from his position high above the stage. Lights reveal more of the space.*

SONG: It's an architectural marvel,
Terrazzo and marble,

> A front desk hewn from Huon pine,
> A counter of kauri,
> A cliff-face of tinted glass,
> Don't be nervous the service is first-world class.

MINH *and the shopping expedition re-enter on the mezzanine level.*

MINH: This way.
OHATSU: Thank you.
MINH: You're welcome.

They and the others continue the song.

SONG: Looking spruce, pining to please,
            There's doormen waiters maitre dees,
            Downstairs kitchen hands are shelling peas.
            We got function rooms and luncheon spreads,
            For conferencees and corporate heads,
            Oversize beds for newly weds,
            A cellar that's strong on whites out of sight for reds!
            No sound from the street,
            Just the air-conditioned quiet of a Hilton or a Hyatt.
            The view you look upon,
            Features beaches—the reaches
            Of the majestic Swan.

High up, PARIS *dons his jacket and prepares to descend.*

SONG: There's to-ing fro-ing, coming going,
            A rooftop pool if you swim,
            A gym if you gym.
            It's a synonym for heaven—the antonym of hell,
            Check in—check out what we sell.
            It's a twenty make that thirty sorry forty storey,
            Five star Perth hotel.

On the mezzanine FOX, MINH *and the* PUPPET OHATSU *run some dialogue. The vamp has continued under.*

FOX: Time and tide wait for no man but we must wait for the lift.
MINH: It's usually quicker from the mezzanine.
FOX: O good, so we're here for a reason.

A final slow, dreamy grab of the song.

SONG: It's a regular / Shangrila / with the / aura / of a / DREAM!

> KEIKO *withdraws. Lights change to just the figures on the mezzanine and a downshaft on* PARIS *as he slowly descends. The* PUPPET OHATSU *sighs.*

FOX: *Skaritta desu ka?*

OHATSU: *Skaritta so desu ne.*

MINH: They speak in Japanese and I lean forward. I speak some Japanese and try to pick up more whenever I can. Was she tired? Yes she is. I got that much.

> MINH *is attached by her costume to the wall, or her feet are in clamps, so that she can 'lean' at weird, non-naturalistic angles.*

OHATSU: Weary. So very weary.

MINH: They were back to English. And I lean back, lest it be thought I'm eavesdropping. Mistakes like that can cost you tips. When the doors open on the other lift this modern day Japanese prince steps towards them. I have to tell her no.

> *The 'other lift' to which* MINH *refers contains* PARIS, *whose descent is halted. He and the* PUPPET OHATSU *exchange a look.* FOX *is looking elsewhere.* MINH *narrates.*

OHATSU: Not going up?

PARIS: I hope not.

OHATSU: Going down?

PARIS: Like my life.

> PARIS *continues his descent.*

MINH: *Shita*—down. *Ue*—up. It's no hindrance I tell you, knowing bits and pieces of a foreign language. Can make the difference between a good tip and nothing. Can make the difference between holding and losing a job in the hospitality trade.

> *Lights are now confined to a section of the mezzanine.* PARIS' *descent has continued into the darkness below.*

She is reaching into her purse and I'm thinking here we go—*Ue Shita*—my bit of Japanese lingo is about to pay a dividend. But no.

Up comes a business card—*are wa meishi desu*—oops, could be overdoing the Japanese.

OHATSU: *Elebeta no hito.* [The man in the lift.]

FOX: *Iya, mimasendeshita yo.* [Didn't see him.]

OHATSU: *Ko no hito dato omou.* [I think it's this man.]

> *She hands* FOX *the business card and they peer down into the foyer.*

Hora koi jaketto o kiteiru. [Look, there below in the dark jacket.]

FOX: *Ar, so no yo desu ne.* [I think you're right, it is him.]

MINH: The guy in the lift is the guy on the card is the guy below seems to be the drift.

> FOX *gives the business card back to the* PUPPET OHATSU.

FOX: *Naze Mark Paris o gozonji nan desuka?* [How do you know Mark Paris?]

MINH: Mark Paris—wow, even I'm surprised, and I'm used to seeing no end of celebs at this hotel I can tell you.

FOX: What's Mark Paris doing on the premises? I'd have thought he'd be persona non grata.

MINH: I'm told he sometimes patronises our Health Club.

FOX: Then you must be running the only club in Perth that'll still have him as a member.

MINH: Apparently he has a life membership.

FOX: Must have bought it when he had a life.

OHATSU: You make him sound like a criminal.

FOX: My dear, with the possible exception of Alan Bond, Mark Paris is the biggest financial deviant this city has ever produced.

OHATSU: After you.

> *Their 'lift' has arrived. They step behind the wall, vacating the mezzanine level. A beat and* MINH*'s head appears from behind the wall to continue her narration.*

MINH: We go '*ue*' one floor when she stops the lift and she's out of there.

> *The* PUPPET OHATSU *reappears.*

OHATSU: I've forgotten something, I won't be long.

MINH: I can take you down.

OHATSU: I'll use the stairs, it's easier.

MINH: To the left and to the right.

> *She looks left and right. The puppet's masked operator's head goes one way, the puppet's head the other.*

OHATSU: Thank you.

MINH: You're welcome (hmm, nice arse).

> MINH *watches the* PUPPET OHATSU *exit, then withdraws her head behind the wall. A beat and her head reappears.*

No skin off my nose this stopping and starting but we go no real distance and it's his turn to bring the vehicle to a halt.

> FOX *steps from the lift, cursing.*

FOX: She wouldn't, would she?

MINH: Asked such questions I try to remain non-committal.

FOX: My God, Mark Paris. How the mighty have fallen. What floor are we?

MINH: Now? Ten.

FOX: Can we go down?

> FOX *returns to the lift.*

MINH: Of course. (In this game you try and tell people what they want to hear but, having pressed the up button, I know we'll be going up first, before coming down.)

> MINH *withdraws into the lift. A shift in the music marks the appearance, below, of the* PUPPET PARIS. OHATSU *steps from the band area, her puppet self having, for the moment, gone. She observes the* PUPPET PARIS *from a distance.* PARIS *enters to the band area* OHATSU *left in order to speak the dialogue for the* PUPPET PARIS. *He seems to read the lines from a magazine as he turns the pages. He, too, represents a bunraku narrator in the same way as* OHATSU *had. The* DANCER *as the ghost of* KEIKO *holds up a newspaper for the* PUPPET PARIS *to scan.*

PARIS: What's this the year 2000 the millennium approaches bullshit the papers are full of?

OHATSU: She sees him across the hotel lobby, sees him stopped by the hotel newsstand.

PARIS: Every newspaper every second magazine every lunatic on the circuit giving us the drum, telling us what a milestone in world history the year 2000 represents.

OHATSU: I'll wait she thinks. Apparently he's talking to someone.

PARIS: The millennium's a Christian event—2000 years since Christ was born. What's that likely to mean to a Muslim, a Buddhist, a Hindu?

OHATSU: Drawing closer she notes a quite fierce debate is being waged.

PARIS: Save me save me save me.

OHATSU: Was debate the wrong word? Was prayer more like it?

PARIS: Save me from this figment of the Euro-American imagination.

OHATSU: The talk gets even louder.

PARIS: Save me from the arrogance of this delusion, this exercise in self-importance. Save me above all from the drivel the daily press daily pours into my poor, addled brain.

OHATSU: Closer now she is fascinated by how animated Mark Paris seems, but who is he talking to?

PARIS: Come the big year they really will be getting off their bikes about it in China, won't they? There they date the year how? From Peking man? From the Ming from the Tang? Or is Mao's ascension the key, from 1949, so 2000's gonna be 51 PM, post Mao. Has the whiff of a big party that one. The millennium is upon us! Which us?

> OHATSU *is closer now. The puppet has taken her in.*

In Japan they date the year by the length of an Emperor's reign—so 2000'll be what? Heisei ten or Heisei eleven—a very momentous sounding event that is. In seven eighths of the known world the millennium is an utterly foreign, forgettable temporal concept. Not here in Perth—here it's news, laid on like tap water. No—bore water.

OHATSU: Suddenly she realises he's talking to no-one—to thin air.

PARIS: My God.

OHATSU: Something he too seems to realise.

PARIS: I'm doing it again—yaketty yak. More and more of late he was losing it. At home alone it didn't matter, but in public? This was getting to be a very untenable habit. Had anyone heard?

> *The operator's head looks one way, the* PUPPET PARIS *looks another.* OHATSU, KEIKO *and* PARIS *also 'look around'.*

OHATSU: Someone is at one of the hotel pay phones—have they overheard him?

PARIS: Seemingly not.

OHATSU: At the front desk a couple are checking in—have they, have the staff seen all this?

PARIS: Again seemingly not. Had he even been talking out loud? That was the hell of it. You crossed over into this nightmare state, you only knew you'd been there because you were back. Would that be his lot? He'd slip off one day and not come back. Someone definitely was looking at him, he could sense it, feel it.

OHATSU: Do you often do that?

> OHATSU *is close to the puppet now.* PARIS *steps from the band area into the foyer.*

PARIS: Do what?

> OHATSU *looks across to him. The* PUPPET PARIS *and operator exit on a musical sting. So does* KEIKO. OHATSU *looks back to where the puppet was. It's gone. Undeterred by the 'vanishing act', she addresses* PARIS.

OHATSU: Do you often talk to yourself?

PARIS: It's the medication.

OHATSU: You're on medication?

PARIS: Yes. No. The lack of medication. I'm not but perhaps I should be. An amazing thing, human consciousness.

OHATSU: I can but agree.

PARIS: I fall into these patterns of free association. I only know I'm doing it when I return.

OHATSU: To the real world?

PARIS: How real is real? Excuse me. I'll drive the lunatic home.

OHATSU: Please don't go.

> PARIS *has started to move away, but stops.*

PARIS: Pardon?

OHATSU: I said please don't go.

PARIS: Why?

OHATSU: Because for me this is something of a miracle.

PARIS: A miracle? I thought I was the loopy one. If miracles exist I'll have three—in fact I could use a dozen.

OHATSU: The first Australian I ever met—here I am in Perth—and bingo our paths cross. You do recognise me, don't you?

PARIS: You were waiting for a lift not two or three minutes ago.

OHATSU: And?

PARIS: And what?

OHATSU: And six years ago, almost to the day, I showed you around my city. Osaka.

PARIS: That I don't remember.

OHATSU: That I don't forget. Faces are a strength of mine.

PARIS: Alas, these days I'm fast becoming the man who mistook his wife for a hat.

OHATSU: How is your wife?

PARIS: My wife's left me but my hat's in good shape. Osaka is going back.

OHATSU: You were selling my father parcels of bonds.

PARIS: Alan Bonds? A bad joke. In poor taste.

OHATSU: Sushi bonds they were termed, essentially a way of avoiding my country's foreign investment regulations. For my father they proved a less than wise investment.

PARIS: Is that right?

OHATSU: I've something here that may jog your memory.

She ferrets in her bag for the business card.

PARIS: Listen, if this is a cute way of serving a writ forget it—I'm already bankrupt.

OHATSU: Bankrupt?

PARIS: There's an edge to the way she says it.

OHATSU: I think we're all that one way or another, don't you?

PARIS: It stops him leaving.

OHATSU: This is your card, is it not?

She hands it to him.

PARIS: Mark Paris, eh? But did he want to admit it? Did he have time for this—for her, for this hotel, this city?

OHATSU: This intrusion—you don't welcome it?

PARIS: Was she reading his mind or was he—yet again—speaking his thoughts aloud? I hate to disillusion you. People have remarked on the resemblance between myself and Mark Paris, but I'm not who you think.

OHATSU: Why lie?

PARIS: Am I lying? And if I am, I'd have thought your sense of Japanese etiquette would allow me to get away with it.

OHATSU: Three years in New York have made me rather un-Japanese. Of course if you have somewhere to be—but if not, a coffee, or a drink would be nice.

PARIS: For why?

OHATSU: For auld lang syne.

PARIS: Now you're the one who's lying.

OHATSU: Alright—because for six years I've carried within me the all but certain knowledge that we two would meet at least one more time before I died. How's that sound? I consider such feelings precious because they run deep, and think they should be heeded.

PARIS: And if I still insist I'm not Mark Paris?

OHATSU: Then, assuming it's not too late, the real Mark Paris can expect a phone call from me tonight—or tomorrow—or the next day, or the next.

They face each other. Above them, the head of MINH *reappears from behind the wall.*

MINH: Having gone *ue* quite a few floors, and come *shita* only slowly, the cavalry arrives.

FOX *steps from the lift onto the mezzanine.*

FOX: This is the mezzanine. I wanted the ground.

MINH: Sorry, I wasn't thinking.

FOX: You're not the only one not thinking.

MINH: I must have pressed—

FOX: Where is she?

MINH: The wrong button.

FOX: There she is.

MINH: And she was—

FOX: Damn it.

MINH: With Mark Paris.

FOX: Ohatsu-san. Ohatsu-san. I really must insist you come away from that man.

PARIS: I recognise that voice.

OHATSU: I call him the fox, a) because it's his name, b) because he looks like one.

PARIS: I call him the dingo, a) because he'd eat babies, except b) he's far too busy selling grandmothers by milking his firm's trust fund.

OHATSU: I know I don't trust him.

PARIS: What—not trust a respected lawyer?

OHATSU: Isn't that—

PARIS: I think it is.

OHATSU: A contradiction in terms—

PARIS: An oxymoron.

FOX: You're the moron, pal.

PARIS: Be careful—I'll sue.

FOX: I'd have said Mark Paris has put himself beyond all reasonable recourse to the law.

OHATSU: Well at least that's cleared something up. The gentleman has been telling me he's not Mark Paris.

FOX: Of course he is—and if you want to commit social suicide my dear, then being seen with him is the best way I know of doing it. In this city tongues wag.

MINH: I thought it was tails that wagged and tongues—

A look from FOX.

Did something else.

OHATSU: He's been lying, no doubt to save me the embarrassment of being seen with him. Seems you've rather ruined his ruse.

FOX: I have?

PARIS: Just when you think chivalry is dead, up I bob. Ohatsu, is it?

OHATSU: It is.

PARIS: In an ideal world I'd offer to buy you a drink, alas.

FOX: What? Not got the ready cash. I am surprised.

OHATSU: I think I can stand an old acquaintance a drink. Please tell my father.

FOX: Tell your father what?

OHATSU: That I've met an old friend and I'll be along soon.

FOX: Will I tell him which old friend?

OHATSU: Why don't I leave that to your better judgement.

FOX: It should be left to someone's—yours has clearly gone astray. I really must counsel you against such a move.

OHATSU: You may counsel my father, Mr Fox, but thankfully your jurisdiction doesn't extend to my personal affairs.

MINH: And that's more or less where the story ended from my point of view. Well almost.

FOX: You know what you look like, you look like a piece of fucking wedding cake.

MINH: Here we go. And you'd like to eat me. The shit you put up with in this job.

> FOX *and* MINH *stand there as the wall shifts across them like a lift door closing. Music and lighting signal a change to the piano bar. The bar moves forward from under the mezzanine. It's the domain of a large puppet,* ALBERT, *the barman, who is behind the bar. (This puppet is operated and voiced from within.)* PARIS *and* OHATSU *move towards two bar stools.*

PARIS: The hotel's piano bar is a bar I used to frequent. These days I confine myself to using the fitness facilities here.

ALBERT: Though few here consider him a fit person.

PARIS: We'd like a drink dead-head. I should be saying welcome to Perth. All I can say is welcome to my nightmare.

ALBERT: Will that be cash, Mr Paris?

PARIS: Albert's a part of that nightmare. He's had trouble with me before.

OHATSU: I'll be ordering the drinks.

ALBERT: I can serve the lady—I can't serve the scumbag.

OHATSU: A whiskey?

PARIS: Perfect.

OHATSU: Two whiskies. Twenty-two eleven.

ALBERT: Is that the time—doesn't it fly?

OHATSU: It's my family's suite. Room two two one one.

ALBERT: O. So you'll be signing for this?

OHATSU: I'm a guest.

ALBERT: But can I trouble you for a signature?

PARIS: You want her to sign for two drinks she hasn't received?

OHATSU: Is there a problem?

ALBERT: I'll need to clear it with my supervisor.

PARIS: I'm the problem.

OHATSU: If that's the rule.

ALBERT: It is when you're with him.

PARIS: Albert you're a worm.

ALBERT: My hands are tied.

> OHATSU *has signed a chit and put it in* ALBERT's *hand. He collapses into an inanimate state.*

PARIS: See—a leper, a social pariah, no better than a Bali dog. This is happening because you're with me.

OHATSU: And the last time I was with you? What happened then?

PARIS: You're the one with the memory.

OHATSU: Is the past for you a country you don't want to return to even though you once lived there?

PARIS: That's a way of putting it.

OHATSU: Funny isn't it, meeting up again.

> *The* PUPPET PARIS *and the* PUPPET OHATSU *enter from either side. They meet, almost ceremonially, in the middle and move towards the bar stools.*

PARIS: Ohatsu of Osaka.

OHATSU: Paris from Perth. I liked that joke at the time.

PARIS: Was it my joke?

OHATSU: No, mine. My English back then was schoolgirlish, and to even make a joke in English was an achievement.

PARIS: A schoolgirl and they'd met in Osaka. Osaka narrowed it down—but Ohatsu as a name rang no bells.

OHATSU: I'm not offended. It's not a crime if you don't remember me. It's not as if we were lovers.

> PARIS *and* OHATSU *stand to sing a duet, ceding the bar stools to their puppet selves.*

SONG: It's her holiday in Spain,
         How the country's needing rain,
         How she used to wear her hair,
         Small talk.
         It's that person over there,
         It's the weather it's the time.
         How I'm afraid I'm going grey,

Small talk.
And all the talk is small—but hey,
All the talk is small—but hey,
Small talk has a way
Of being all you need to say.

The piano bar vamp continues under. PARIS *and* OHATSU *have now, in effect, become narrators to the actions of the puppets. The small talk resumes.*

OHATSU: Chikamatsu Monzaemon, *Sonezaki Shinju*, 1703.

PARIS: That's the name of the puppet play you took me to?

OHATSU: The name of the writer, the play, and the date it was written.

The PUPPET PARIS *scratches his head—he can't recall such a play.*

We always took foreign visitors to such things. The bunraku, the Takarazuka, even the yose and the sumo. That night my mother had a prior engagement. I took her place, chaperoned by my brother of course.

PARIS: And after the puppet play?

OHATSU: We ate.

PARIS: Aussie beef?

OHATSU: Shabu shabu—but it may have been Aussie beef—you have a memory of Aussie beef?

PARIS: No. I just like saying it.

The PUPPET OHATSU *laughs behind her hand.*

OHATSU: We ate, we went on to a live house—a local Osakan heavy metal band—my brother and I wanted to show our important foreign visitor how 'with it' Osaka really was. No memory of that either, moving right along. We walked and small-talked our way through Dotonbori.

PARIS: With your brother?

OHATSU: No. I'd paid him to stay at the club.

PARIS: You had designs on me?

OHATSU: I'm not saying. We stopped by a bridge. Ya Tigers! I told you about the local baseball team. How when it lost people jumped off this bridge. No? Boy. I'm really playing hot pachinko tonight.

PARIS: Let's start again with the puppet play, we're there in our seats.

OHATSU: Not seats, the tatami section.

> *On the mezzanine level, the ghost of* KEIKO *enters. She carries an oblong square of tatami to illustrate the story and, sitting above, she looks down on the bar. Again the pose suggests a bunraku narrator flanking the action.*

PARIS: Ar yes, life in the corporate box.

OHATSU: You remember it now?

PARIS: I remember tatami, sitting on tatami.

OHATSU: The hotel room was tatami, maybe you're remembering that.

PARIS: The hotel?

OHATSU: My friend Keiko—poor Keiko—very wicked of us really— unknown to our parents we shared the rent on a room in a small hotel. I took you there.

PARIS: And?

OHATSU: We drank some more, laughed a lot, at one point—wicked of me but I remember it—I drew my naked foot across your throat.

> *The* PUPPET OHATSU *makes a throat cutting gesture.*

Like the heroine in the play we'd seen. I explained how that was a sign. She was expressing her readiness to die with her lover, it's a very famous scene, but you don't—

PARIS: I'm sorry—

OHATSU: Remember. I'm not offended.

PARIS: She says it again.

OHATSU: I'm not offended.

PARIS: But she can't mask the disappointment in her voice.

OHATSU: Like I said, we weren't lovers or anything.

PARIS: But it is like she expects from him something he hasn't the power to give.

> *The* PUPPET PARIS *picks up the business card from the bar. Above,* KEIKO *turns the tatami square, revealing a larger scale version of the same business card on the reverse side.*

I should update this card shouldn't I, let's see.

OHATSU: He tries to make light of the situation.

PARIS: Am I still Mark Paris, yes, that's established, and more's the pity. My title, company secretary, you can scrub that, and scrub the company, it's kaput, but I guess you know about the 80s.

OHATSU: In Japan we call it the bubble economy.

PARIS: The bubble economy?

OHATSU: It burst.

PARIS: The home address is intact, I'm still there though for how long remains to be seen. The wife and the creditors are fighting over who's entitled to the title. While they keep fighting I maintain my status as the idiot in residence. The phone? Optus are threatening disconnection but so far so good. All this is in Japanese, isn't it, on the back.

The PUPPET PARIS *turns the card over and notes something unusual.*

OHATSU: That's Keiko's doing.

PARIS: Your friend?

OHATSU: Yes.

PARIS: And he sees in red biro a heart drawn on an old business card.

Above, KEIKO *also reverses the card and proceeds to draw a heart shape on it with a felt pen.*

OHATSU: Keiko was always teasing me about my foreign lover.

PARIS: Was?

OHATSU: Keiko's dead.

A vocal chorus begins the song which PARIS *and* OHATSU *complete alone.*

SONG: But small talk can get big,
          Small talk can get big,
          It passes time—and that's its art.
          But there's the times it tears the heart
          Apart.
          It's the colour of the room,
          It's the perfume that you bought,
          How you ought to go it's late,
          Small talk.
          Like the clue to eight across,

Has the landlord changed the locks?
More often than his socks,
Small talk.
And all the talk is small—but hey,
All the talk is small—but hey,
Small talk has a way
Of being all you need to say.

The ghost of KEIKO *has gone.* ALBERT *is back behind the bar.*

OHATSU: Ar, our drinks.

PARIS: At last.

ALBERT: There's something of a problem.

PARIS: You love this, don't you Albert?

ALBERT: The room number checks out but the signature isn't kosher.

OHATSU: You mean its not an authorised signature?

ALBERT: Apparently not.

OHATSU: Meaning I can't go to breakfast alone, or order a coffee and cake or a drink unless who—my father or mother sign for it, is that what you're saying?

ALBERT: If you care to go to the front desk, you're welcome to remedy the signature situation with my supervisor.

OHATSU: Why don't I just ring my father?

ALBERT: You're welcome to use the house phone.

OHATSU: I wouldn't want to trouble hotel management—I'll use my mobile.

PARIS: That's got him worried. This'll slow the influx of Japanese visitors to Perth from a torrent to a trickle.

ALBERT: Just doing my job.

PARIS: Just following orders.

The live OHATSU *gets her mobile phone from her bag.*

OHATSU: I hope my mobile's charged.

PARIS: We could all use a charge.

OHATSU: Will cash solve our problem?

PARIS: Cash—the eyes light up.

The PUPPET OHATSU *receives some banknotes from* OHATSU.

ALBERT: Yen?

PARIS: I can't put yen through the till.

ALBERT: Yen?

PARIS: I put yen through the till they put me through the mincer!

ALBERT: You're welcome to change it at the foreign currency exchange booth, it's on the upper level.

PARIS: The eyes glaze over yet again.

ALBERT: No plastic? You'd be—

PARIS: Don't say welcome, Albert, or I'll spew on your shoes.

The PUPPET OHATSU *dials her mobile.*

Years ago I would have punched Albert's dial for something like this. Biff kapow.

He punches ALBERT. *While* PARIS *remains calm, the* PUPPET PARIS *stands, bashes his own head on the bar, waves his arms.*

But I don't do that, do I? Kapow biff. Instead I remain calm and civil. I'm a bankrupt. If I knock heads, I knock my own. I'm a disgraced and notorious figure. It ill behoves someone in my state to cause a public nuisance. I don't make waves. I tug my forelock. I keep my head down. If I offend, I'm only doing what people expect.

The PUPPET OHATSU *is on the phone, waiting for an answer.*

The more I play the monster the greater my already great sins grow in the eyes of my fellow citizens—why make a scene when frankly I wouldn't want to give my fellow citizens that pleasure.

ALBERT: Speaking of your fellow citizens.

PARIS: Aw O.

OHATSU: Strange. No answer. What?

PARIS: Some of the local fauna have arrived. Escapees from the Nedlands and Dalkeith Menagerie. It's a human zoo.

Still on the phone the PUPPET OHATSU *looks around and sees that two figures,* FINN *and* MCSCRAG, *have entered the bar. Both have shark's fins sewn into the back of their costumes. The second sports a dog collar. They already have drinks and remain by the piano.*

ALBERT: The bloke in the lead's Sir Errol Finn.

PARIS: He's in real estate.

ALBERT: The real shark's the bloke behind him.

PARIS: A finance journalist.

ALBERT: A newshound with the *Fin Review*. This one took them both to the cleaners over the Swan Brewery site.

FINN: Nine years.

MCSCRAG: To nine years or more.

> *The* PUPPET PARIS *lowers his head. The* PUPPET OHATSU *puts down the phone. The live actors look at one another, ceasing the narrational focus they've had on the puppets until now.*

OHATSU: Nine years?

PARIS: They're toasting my future. That's the jail term I've been warned to expect.

OHATSU: When?

PARIS: I'm on bail. It's pronounced next week. Like I say: welcome to my nightmare.

OHATSU: Why would I want to be part of your nightmare when I have a nightmare of my own. My family and other animals, she says.

PARIS: Quite the touring party.

> KEIKO *pushes a wheeled costume rack forward. From it are suspended the masks and primitive cut-out bodies of a family group: mother, sister, father, brother-in-law and, behind him, husband-to-be. The* FOX *mask is also amongst them. As* OHATSU *and* PARIS *resume their narration, the* PUPPET OHATSU *and the* PUPPET PARIS *stand from their stools and gesture.*

OHATSU: You will note how we Japanese don't need words to convey our innermost feelings. My mother and sister's eyes speak volumes.

PARIS: Telling you what?

OHATSU: Telling me to do what father says.

PARIS: What of your father, what's he telling you?

OHATSU: The brow is furrowed, yes? This is a matter therefore of great concern. A question of money or family honour is involved.

PARIS: I'd call that brow deeply furrowed.

OHATSU: Then it's a question of money *and* honour.

PARIS: Is that the brother I met?

OHATSU: Alas, my brother didn't make the journey, that's brother-in-law. He and sister are deeply into the joys of wedlock. In their case gridlock's an apter term.

PARIS: And the other bloke?

Another figure, identical to the cut out brother-in-law, folds out from behind the brother-in-law. They are two of a kind, sprung from the same mould.

OHATSU: My husband-to-be. We're in Perth with a view to some time hence spending our honeymoon here.

PARIS: O. So you're to be married, congratulations.

OHATSU: Most people say that.

PARIS: You don't sound overjoyed.

OHATSU: I've not been well of late. Yes father, I'm coming.

The PUPPET OHATSU *and the* PUPPET PARIS *begin a move away from the bar.* OHATSU *and* PARIS *follow, continuing their narration.*

PARIS: No prize for guessing what the execrable Mr Fox thinks of all this—he's put you in it big-time, hasn't he—a grin from ear to ear.

OHATSU: He should be slit from ear to ear.

PARIS: Now, now.

OHATSU: A pity, isn't it? This could have been a light and carefree occasion. Is it proving that? No.

PARIS: Old friends meeting after long years over a drink—but can they get one? No. Can I ask what husband-to-be's face is telling you?

OHATSU: That this, like all things, will pass.

PARIS: That's a comfort.

OHATSU: Isn't it.

The bar scene is melting away. OHATSU *bows towards* PARIS.

Thank you Mr Mark—it's rare for me to meet someone from the old days. A happy event, darkened alas, by the sadness of our separate situations.

PARIS: The way she says it, like a cry from the bottom of her heart, the old days, like they were the good times, whereas now?

OHATSU *and the* PUPPET OHATSU *exit.* PARIS *remains. The rack containing the family grouping goes. The ghost of* KEIKO *remains.*

If a lot of bad had happened to him since they met, what, he wondered, had happened to her. Inside he felt like glass about to shatter.

PARIS *and the* PUPPET PARIS *exit. Enter the* NARRATOR, *no longer a hotel staff member. Accompanied by the band, she starts to sing at a whisper.* KEIKO *pulls the hotel wall across the darkness into which the bar has disappeared. The upper 'lift-hole' is now central, with the lighting's focus on the downstage floor area.* KEIKO *builds her second major dance sequence as the song develops.*

SONG: You gotta give it air (a story),
         Let it breathe (a story),
         Give it room to move,
         Be it tragedy comedy history mystery,
         Satire crime—or romance.

         You gotta set it free (a story),
         Let it run (a story),
         Tie its hands and it stands,
         Trembling with fear a mere house of cards,
         Trapped by the advance,
         Of the coming avalanche.

         If you find it bound unbind it,
         Turn it around unwind it,
         Set it free let it live and you give it a chance,
         If it's alive (a story),
         If it's alive (a story),
         If it's alive it can dance!

The music builds as the dance sequence, featuring KEIKO *and the* NARRATOR, *unfolds. A spotlight suddenly reveals* PARIS, *framed by the open panel above.*

NARRATOR: Suddenly—have the flood-gates of memory opened— Mark Paris is back there, in a house in Osaka and a schoolgirl in a Japanese school uniform is bowing his way.

Used as a puppet, a headless Japanese-style school uniform bows as it enters from under the mezzanine. The schoolgirl OHATSU's *face appears from behind.*

The schoolgirl introduces herself.

OHATSU: I'll be taking mother's place and accompanying you to the theatre tonight. Excuse me. I must change.

The school uniform is again empty of human form. Then it vanishes, replaced by the kimono OHATSU *wore to the theatre the night she met* MARK PARIS. OHATSU*'s face appears from behind the kimono. This is a wordless play of memory for* PARIS *who, in a way, has himself become a puppet.*

NARRATOR: In no time it seems the schoolgirl is back—but in traditional Japanese female attire, the sleeve of her kimono beckoning to him.

OHATSU: The car is ready.

The NARRATOR, *the band, and sound effects echo and distort the words* OHATSU *speaks, creating an eerie atmosphere to the scene.* KEIKO *continues her dance.*

NARRATOR: Were they the words she used then? Or was he making them up now? Was memory up to its old tricks?

OHATSU: My brother will be driving.

NARRATOR: Still he can and can't put a face to this picture—still she does and doesn't elude him.

OHATSU*'s face, behind the kimono, melts into darkness. So does the kimono, revealing* KEIKO *dancing as a 'night club rager'.*

Is that her—in some basement some heaving smoke wreathed underground night spot? Are they together, two wild abandoned creatures dancing with an animal freedom that wrings both breath and sweat from his body? And when she shouts.

YUMI: Osakan heavy metal hey!

NARRATOR: Does he not shout back as he dances—

PARIS: You're Osakan heavy metal.

NARRATOR: And boy, does he means it.

YUMI: What?

NARRATOR: What is what she says because the music is loud.

PARIS: You're Osakan heavy metal!

YUMI: What?

PARIS: You're Osakan heavy metal!

KEIKO*'s dancing figure stops and turns to walk towards* PARIS. *She starts speaking Japanese ("Are you talking to me lover boy?"), tearing at her clothes. Bits of fabric come away in her hands.*

NARRATOR: But it's not her face—was she even wearing that outfit—is he mixing her up with someone else with someone else with—no—that was in Tokyo not Osaka. Or was it Kyoto. No matter, the things he made that woman do hardly made it likely six years later she'd still be carrying his business card.

The tatami square has floated in. So has the headless kimono, which masks OHATSU. *The* PUPPET PARIS *enters.*

The play. A wave of self-disgust is coursing through his guts, a well of black bile so bitter the self-loathing threatens to overcome all sense of balance and send him crashing to the floor. The play—was there anything there—again that kimono beckoning him to her side. He's saying.

PARIS: Where do we sit?

OHATSU: Here on the tatami.

The kimono again has OHATSU's *face behind it. The* PUPPET PARIS *is placed on the tatami square.*

NARRATOR: Is there somewhere in the world a tatami mat that, when you sink into it—it swallows people whole—and all trace is wiped clean, all memory of them and their deeds erased? Would that not be a blessing and a good invention?

Kneeling, the PUPPET PARIS *begins to sink into the tatami square and disappear. As the puppet sinks, the panel in the wall closes across* PARIS *to the strains of another song. Exit the tatami square and the 'disappeared' puppet. The faceless kimono bows and hurries away.*

SONG: Inside he feels like breaking glass,
          He's being told all this will pass.
          But what if all you do is done to last
          A lifetime through?
          It dogs your days,
          It weighs the scales,
          Is that so hard to grasp?

The panel's sliding 'wipes' PARIS *but reveals the* PUPPET OHATSU *on the mezzanine level. She is seated, holding up a tiny doll. Behind her, the puppet figures of her mother and sister seem to tower over her.*

NARRATOR: Elsewhere Ohatsu hears, in the next room, the men in her family, like so many puppets, laughing and jeering as the execrable Fox-san plies them with tale after tale of Mark Paris' infamy. But if they seem like puppets, her mother and sister are like demons.

The NARRATOR *supplies the voices of the mother and sister.*

MOTHER: Is she crazy?

SISTER: Stupid.

MOTHER: Is she crazy?

SISTER: Stupid.

MOTHER: You are not—not—not getting married looking like that.

NARRATOR: I am, she says, I am getting married like that because that is how Keiko looked the night she died.

KEIKO *re-enters, below, holding a doll similar to that held by the* PUPPET OHATSU.

SISTER: Keiko is dead, finished, forget Keiko.

MOTHER: Girls in this family do not—do not—do not get married looking like male impersonators, like some Takarazuka superstar, do you want husband-to-be to think you're crazy?

SISTER: Stupid.

MOTHER: Crazy.

SISTER: Stupid.

MOTHER: Give me that doll.

NARRATOR: No!

MOTHER: Ar, Fox-san.

The mask representing FOX *re-appears on the costume rack.*

FOX: I'll take my leave. *Itte mairimasu.*

MOTHER: *Itte rasshai.* You speak such good Japanese.

FOX: Do I?

SISTER: Doesn't he?

NARRATOR: And as the women show the family's ever so clever Australian friend out, Ohatsu sinks deeper into herself. I'll take the air on the balcony, she says.

The mother, daughter and FOX *exit as the wall panel begins to slide across the* PUPPET OHATSU. *The song is repeated.*

SONG: Inside she feels like breaking glass,

> She's being told all this will pass,
> But what if all you do is done to last,
> A lifetime through?
> It dogs your days,
> It weighs the scales,
> Is that so hard to grasp?

To the sounds of the shamisen, OHATSU *comes into view at the other edge of the mezzanine. Framed by the 'lift-hole', she is seated on a stair unit. She wears a kimono and is binding her fan to a broomstick. This is the puppet character from* Sonezaki Shinju, *although played by the live actress. As the wall panel continues to pass, the stair unit moves further into the space. The 'lift-hole' in the wall comes to rest in the centre of the mezzanine where it frames the* PUPPET OHATSU *as she views the 'play'.*

NARRATOR: Suddenly the world of *Sonezaki Shinju* is racing through her head. The reason why is no surprise. It isn't just because she's met Mark Paris again years after they'd seen the puppet play together. It is because, like the heroine in that play, she wants to escape what has become for her an absurd and intolerable situation. Mother, father, sister, brother-in-law, and husband-to-be.

A scene from Sonezaki Shinju *begins to take material form below. It features live performers playing the parts of the puppets from the original play.* KEIKO *plays the maid. The live* OHATSU *plays her namesake.* PARIS *plays Tokubei.*

From the balcony she sees the play itself as though in pure space. Sees the heroine of *Sonezaki Shinju.* Sees her at the top of the stairs. Sees the face of her lover Tokubei in his hiding place under the porch. Sees the maid sleeping below the stairs. And the night lantern shining brightly.

The NARRATOR *holds up a lamp which she will extinguish.*

O the courage and cunning of the heroine. With her fan tied to a broom she tries to reach and extinguish the lamp, attempts it once, twice, and at last does so, but in the process tumbles down the stairs herself. What was that, cries the master of the house.

VOICE: Ohatsu. Father wants to see you.

NARRATOR: Servants! The night lamp's gone out. Wake and light it! It's pitch black, grumbles the maid.

VOICE: He's pretty angry with you.

NARRATOR: Hurry up! I can't find the flint box, says the maid as she searches the room, with the lovers moving this way and that to dodge her. At the entranceway they unfasten the latch but the hinges creak, and frightened by the noise they hesitate. Just then the maid begins to strike the flints. The lovers time their actions to the rasping sounds, and with each rasp open the door further and further.

They are, in fact, pulling it towards them near the stair unit. Above, the PUPPET OHATSU *is moving to stay in the frame the 'lift-hole' provides.*

And, just as the lamp lights up, they make good their escape—and flee from all earthly bondage.

Blackout on the scene from the puppet play. The lovers have gone. The maid is again by the stairs. The NARRATOR *remains. The* PUPPET OHATSU *remains. The movement of the wall panel has revealed the* PUPPET PARIS *at floor level at the other end of the mezzanine.*

In the carpark, looking back and up at the hotel, Paris thinks he sees something. Ohatsu high up on a balcony. He senses a terrible thing is to occur. She'll fall, that's what he thinks. But is it—she is moving away—was it even her?

The PUPPET OHATSU *turns away. The wall panel slowly slides across her as a third version of the song is sung.*

SONG: Inside they feel like breaking glass,
         They're being told all this will pass,
         But what if all you do is done to last,
         A lifetime through?
         It dogs your days,
         It weighs the scales,
         Is that so hard to grasp?

As the wall panel passes, the stair unit moves forward and comes to rest against the wall, helping define it as outside rather than inside the hotel. Moving from the stairs, KEIKO, *no longer the maid, approaches the* PUPPET PARIS. *She holds the Takarazuka doll towards him.*

NARRATOR: But something is falling. Has the wind caught a hotel guest's washing, a child's kite, some junk mail, bringing it now to earth.

As KEIKO *hands the Takarazuka doll to the* PUPPET PARIS, *it is snatched away and replaced by a sheet of newspaper.*

A tiny Japanese doll—no—wouldn't you know it—a page from the *Fin Review* is blowing against his leg.

A light picks out SIR ERROL FINN *and the newshound* MCSCRAG *in the band area. They are relieving themselves against the grand piano. For the time being, the shamisen is the featured instrument.*

FINN: Which car do you think is his? The BMW you're pissing on?

MCSCRAG: No no, Paris always drove Audis.

FINN: An Audi? Maybe it's the one I'm pissing on.

NARRATOR: His enemies knew he was in the carpark. They were looking straight at him, but through him, past him. He was being given the silent treatment. Spoken of—but not to. Paris was used to such tactics, this studied ignoring of his presence.

FINN: Hang on, this can't be Paris' Audi. Bankrupts don't run to luxury cars.

MCSCRAG: That's right. Law is they're expected to live on a more modest scale.

FINN: His car would have to be that 60s Holden parked across the road.

NARRATOR: How right you are, says Paris.

PARIS' *voice is heard, speaking the dialogue together with the* NARRATOR.

FINN: Did you hear something?

MCSCRAG: The wind?

FINN: An early model Holden. Probably the very car, appropriate don't you think?

MCSCRAG: I do, a suitably ramshackle rundown conveyance for filth such as him.

NARRATOR: Filth I may be, shouts Paris, but if I'm filth, am I not filth surrounded by filth? Filth at swim in a sea of filth, an ocean of filth, of ever-present human greed and corruption, of bankruptcy, of venality and degradation so widespread and so deep-running the mind reels back astounded by the horror both within oneself, and within all humankind.

MCSCRAG: The wind again.

FINN: Again the wind—should we go piss on the Holden?

MCSCRAG: Too far to walk.

> *The* PUPPET PARIS *comes forward.*

NARRATOR: They leave, but even then this encounter with his enemies is far from over.

> FINN *and* MCSCRAG *are gone. As* KEIKO *pulls the wall panel into alignment with the mezzanine,* PARIS *is revealed at floor level. The 'lift-hole' is now above the staircase. The puppeteer removes his hood and adopts the character of* GAVIN, *whilst continuing to 'operate' the* PUPPET PARIS, *with support from the second puppeteer (a variation on the ventriloquist and doll routine).* PARIS *observes the scene, providing the dialogue for his puppet self. The* NARRATOR *and* KEIKO *pause for a moment near* PARIS *before departing. A bitter confrontation develops.*

GAVIN: Why don't you die?

PARIS: You never give up, do you.

GAVIN: Why don't you just die?

PARIS: The stalker—Gavin Walker—I see him here, I see him there, I see young Gavin everywhere.

GAVIN: If my presence reminds you of your guilt, then I am content.

PARIS: And I've got places to be.

GAVIN: Then you'll probably need these.

> GAVIN *displays a set of car keys, but keeps them.* PARIS *pats his pockets.*

PARIS: Where'd you get my car keys?

GAVIN: Your jacket, while you were in the gym.

PARIS: YOU didn't steal them, not young Gavin.

GAVIN: A rush of blood. Why not pinch his car I thought, drive it to the Yanchep Estate, set fire to it.

PARIS: Dear, O dear.

GAVIN: Then I thought why stoop to his level? What is this fitness thing, you—jogging in the morning, the gym by night.

PARIS: You do keep an eye on me, don't you?

GAVIN: Trying to muscle up so you can look after yourself in jail? That really will be survival of the fittest in there won't it?

PARIS: Now that's something. What are you going to do for an interest when I'm out of circulation? Who will you haunt and hound then? Your life'll be meaningless, won't it, with me in jail?

GAVIN: I'll visit.

PARIS: You wouldn't.

GAVIN: Why not?

PARIS: I'll refuse to see you—I'll be within my rights—I'll probably have more rights in there than out here.

GAVIN: I'll use the names of people you wouldn't mind seeing, old friends.

PARIS: Do I have any left?

GAVIN: If need be I'll use your children's names. Desperate to see them, you'll front the visitors' room and there I'll be—still haunting you, my presence, as always, a reminder of your guilt.

PARIS: And you know what I'll do, Gavin? I'll happily greet you, all smiles. You'll be astonished what a model prisoner I'm proving to be.

GAVIN: Don't make me laugh.

PARIS: I'll probably take up painting, give you a work or two. I'll tell you about the computer courses I'm doing, the languages I'm learning, how I'm such a favourite with the warders they take me out for cappuccinos, that's the kind of all round good guy I'll be. Better still, as with a small child, I'll lay out the real nature of existence for you, Gavin, like a Mormon at your door, like a Buddhist with a Dali Lama-like grin I'll explain how I am, a grain at a time, like sand, piling up my good deeds—and how in a hundred years there'll be a hill. And there I'll stand looking down on my crimes below, and back on all my folly, and at that moment I'll experience, Gavin, a kind of release.

GAVIN: Sure.

PARIS: But what of you, my friend? Is it not already like a cancer gnawing at your guts? Will it not by then have hollowed you out completely? After 100 years, how far below and how far back will you and your haunting be, how consumed will you be by revenge by then?

GAVIN: My parents. Two elderly people. Their life savings gone. Sleeping pills.

PARIS: They were greedy.

GAVIN: They were misinformed by a false prospectus.

PARIS: Greedy, and heard only what they wanted to hear.

GAVIN: Why don't you die, uh? Why don't you?

> GAVIN *runs the* PUPPET PARIS *back against the staircase. Still gripping it he drags the puppet part way up the stairs, where he lets it go. It lies on the staircase.* GAVIN *climbs towards the exit, above. He pauses.*

Sorry. Your keys.

> *He drops them to the ground. The puppet remains inert.*

PARIS: You poufter! You fag! You greasy dumb wog.

GAVIN: Who are you calling a wog—who changed their name from Padereski to Paris when they arrived in Perth from Kalgoorlie? Drive carefully.

PARIS: I always drive to stay alive.

GAVIN: Don't run into a tree or anything.

PARIS: I wouldn't want to deprive you of your sport, sport.

> PARIS *picks up the car keys before strapping himself into his car seat. Above,* GAVIN *exits. The* PUPPET PARIS *stirs on the staircase. Hurt but defiant, it starts to crawl up the stairs.*

It's never die you cunt with you is it, it's never die you low life snivelling scumbag, die you cock sucking mother fucking root rat, just die why don't you.

> *Lights highlight* PARIS, *barrelling along a highway in his car. Music mixes with the sounds of the car and the voices of an announcer and newsreader on the car radio.*

RADIO: [*announcer's voice*] 10.10 on Triple J coming your way across W.A. [*Newsreader's voice*] Daryl Chittick, 19, died this morning in the front yard of his parents' Kalgoorlie home.

PARIS: Kalgoorlie.

RADIO: [*newsreader's voice*] He'd recently lost his licence, and feeling a life without a car was no life at all, Daryl committed suicide. His friends are advised the funeral will be held on Wednesday next, 11 a.m., at St Mark's church, Boulder. [*Announcer's voice*] No folks, it's not the news, it's from a goldfields band called Deep Lead.

A variety of weird automobile sound effects are mixed in.

Clock that guitar for grit, listen to the grunt of that gearbox. A quirky offering that might just get this band out of the goldfields.

PARIS: Tell 'em not to bother.

RADIO: [*announcer's voice*] And into the big time.

PARIS: I got out of the goldfields. Out of the goldfields and into the fields of gold. Fat lot of good it did me!

RADIO: [*announcer's voice*] What do you think, Celia? 'Lurve at first hear—everyone's singing it Deb'.

When the song lyric cuts in, PARIS *is singing as he drives along.*

SONG: He turns on the wipers then wipes himself out,
      It isn't even raining,
      With a gun between his knees,
      There's nothing worth explaining.
      The radio he's turned it on,
      The radio keeps saying:
      What does it matter this is the end,
      You're going much too fast through a hairpin bend,
      No-one will miss you, you never had a friend,
      They loved you for your car,
      They loved you for your car.

PARIS' *car seat starts to slowly rise. A puppet-scale car crosses the forestage, its lights blazing. On the 'record' the voice of Daryl's mother or his girlfriend is heard.*

RADIO: [*mother's voice*] Why'd you do it Daryl—why'd you do it? Why'd you do it Daryl—why'd you do it?

SONG: At no miles per hour he thumbs the lighter in,
      There's lots he couldn't figure,
      And soon it will pop out,
      Then it's time to pull the trigger.

The radio it's coming on,
Top sound but it's a snigger,
What does it matter this is the end,
You're going much too fast through a hairpin bend,
No-one will miss you, you never had a friend,
They loved you for your car,
They loved you for your car.

PARIS *is now high above the stage. He pushes the radio and there's a change of song. The lighting changes. As he descends, the wall panel begins to move across him, framing him in the 'lift-hole', before he disappears from view. A big ensemble number develops, featuring a third dance sequence from* KEIKO.

SONG: Castles in the air who lives there?
          How long can you drowse
          In the housing
          Of dreamland.
          Success smells sweet,
          Is it ever complete,
          If all you count is the beans
          Of beanland?
          Is that our lot we gotta spot in an in-between-land?

          The real—the imagined / will either ever do,
          Is that the story / is drama / is karma a never done sum,
          A one plus one—that never gets to two?
          Reality's bedrock has a headlock over dream,
          Is the battle fought there?
          Are we caught there?
          The unwise fall-guys meat in the sandwich in between,
          Is history that? A shoji screen,
          Sliding on a track that runs between
          Actuality—Fantasy.
          Which cat gets the cream?
          We see the way the world is,
          We wish for a world that's never been,
          Will that circle ever be squared? What a scene!
          Such a business! The isness of things,

Compared to our imaginings,
In a paper boat we float we sail our hope
Across a troubled sea.

During the song, the movement of the wall reveals PARIS *at ground level. He comes forward to directly address the audience.*

PARIS: Come on you good people of Perth, let's get Mark Paris, let's play get me! And let there be no reprieve, let's leave no stone unturned. It's slash and burn, it's pump gas into the underground warren of my decade of deceit! And why not? I agree. What a financial deviant, what a fiscal pervert. I'm the Goth I'm the vandal I'm the Hun! What haven't I done? I have raped the tax laws. With false prospectus after false prospectus, using every known loophole I have wrecked homes, I have ruined friendships, crushed families, come this close to sinking banks. As with a chain saw I have severed the limbs of pensioners. Thanks to me children have been yanked out of good private schools. Penury and ruin have I visited upon the land. Hang me draw me quarter me slaughter me—have I not done the fiscal equivalent of sticking lit penny bungers up cats' bums?! Burst my bubble, put a bullet through my skull. Nail me jail me let me be your plastic Jesus! And then what?

Throughout this dialogue, a number of props have been set on the floor near PARIS. *They include a rifle, a tripod and the barrel of a telescope (though it could be a bazooka). At mezzanine level* KEIKO *guides the pool ladder into place. Figures carry* PARIS *back to the ladder.*

Then the 80s will be over, right? Give me a break! And what was my crime again? O yes, I made money, I was a big success! Get fucking real!

This fiscal Christ hangs there. The top half of the hotel wall folds slowly over PARIS. *Now reversed, the 'lift-hole' leaves him visible. A side wall is added.*

SONG: Are we the thing the act,
         Or the shadow the mere depiction?
         Are we a friend of fact,
         Or the chaperone of fiction?

Is it an either or / a neither or / a both:
As if a myth can be for us a mathematical proof,
Look how often we soften the truth?
It's like born we learn to lie in the cradle,
Yet grow to know we'll slumber (years without number)
In a grave.
We swim we sink but having swum we finally come to see
Reality's the ship we sail we row and it keeps going.
But does the rowing make us living slaves?
Or is the oar we're given giving us a way
Of making waves!

All is in readiness for Act Two.

END OF ACT ONE

ACT TWO

FOREPLAY

The basic set is an in-ground swimming pool, low lights set in the walls, etc. PARIS *leaves the ladder to come downstage to where the props have been left. Almost counter-weighted by his movement,* OHATSU *enters to the pool deck amongst the skeleton framework that had supported the hotel wall and is now a 'dream home'. She occupies a still position.* OHATSU *and* PARIS *sing together, although they are in different realities.*

SONG: When you can't face the night—but the day has no sun,
          When there's no place to rest—or run,
          When the threat's out there—but also inside,
          Where do you go? Or hide?

The ghost of KEIKO *joins* OHATSU. *They stare into the wings. Downstage, a light, hung from the tripod, has snapped on to illume* PARIS *as he works, cleaning a gun. The song focuses him. A chorus sings.*

SONG: At the deep end of an empty pool,
          With a pull-through and a reaming tool,
          By the light of a lamp stands a man,
          Got a gun in his hand—but is he a man,
          Or is he a fool?

Instrumental underscore continues. The NARRATOR *and two other shadowy chorus figures have surrounded* PARIS. *They have been at work assembling, then disassembling the pieces of the gun, the tripod body, the eye-piece of the telescope, etc. The image of objects forming up, coming from disassembly into complete array, is a key image. These black hooded stage management figures echo Japanese theatre tradition in their assistance with props and the focus they give the live characters. They create a sense almost of ritual, avoiding the fussy naturalism of actors dealing with objects. Meanwhile, on the deck,* OHATSU *remains in a fixed position. Possibly* KEIKO *supplies essential non-musical sound effects, eg. walking on gravel. There is a sandbox, door chimes, etc, for her to operate.*

NARRATOR: And the man hears a car pull up in the street outside, hears a car door open and later shut, hears a snatch of a taxi's radio, hears the purr of an engine idling. As the taxi drives off, as the noise of its engine fades, he hears footsteps clicking across concrete, hears the creak of a gate, hears those same footsteps coming down a gravel walk, hears the ringing of a front door bell. Who, he wonders, would be visiting him, this late at night?

PARIS reaches out to turn the tripod light off. Is he thinking this visitor might be an enemy? Apparently so. There's now just the spill from the lighting of the pool. The three black figures shrink against the pool walls: a tension, a sense of expectancy held in their bodies. One, for example, is twined around the steel pool ladder. Heads incline towards the sound. The doorbell's chime stops.

PARIS: It wouldn't be? No. Not twice in one night.

A brief slash of light illuminates the face of GAVIN, *the creditor stalker.*

NARRATOR: Paris hears the footsteps start up, but not retreating, getting closer, down the side of the house they come, across the deck that flanks the pool, towards the back door of the house this man once owned but now merely occupies.

OHATSU *crosses the pool deck in silhouette She reaches out as though to knock on a door. Suddenly, from above, a light shaft pins her in profile.* PARIS *talks to her but doesn't turn to face her.*

PARIS: Don't be alarmed.

She freezes. The figures in the pool freeze. KEIKO *is observing him.*

It's the security system. You've triggered it. But don't speak—let me guess.

PARIS *is standing, looking into the auditorium. He holds the rifle, having assembled it in case this was an unwanted intruder. He lists the clues.*

Clue number one: From the footsteps I'd say you're female—but not my wife—I know her cat-like tread. Nor, having banned me from visiting her and the children, would she lightly return to the scene of our not so joyous domestic bliss. Then there's the car you came in: clue number two. I know what the car she'd be using sounds like—I ought to—it used to be mine.

OHATSU *has slowly turned to look towards* PARIS *at the far end of the pool. For the moment she doesn't see the gun because* PARIS *has his back to her. She is 'surprised' to find him in the pool (and that the pool is empty) but 'acts' this surprise in a low-key manner. It's a slo-mo moment.*

A taxi suggests what? A visitor to Perth? Perhaps, humour me please, a blast from my past, come back to haunt me, could it be the ghost of a Japanese Princess—eeek it is.

PARIS *has turned and is facing her.*

OHATSU: Not a ghost, flesh and—
NARRATOR: And she sees the gun. She sees the gun and she thinks.
OHATSU: No.
NARRATOR: But stops that thought before it starts—she sees the gun and tries to make light of it.
OHATSU: Also part of the security arrangements?
PARIS: You could say that.
OHATSU: Would anyone believe you?
NARRATOR: She sees the gun and not wanting to express her shock she simply observes that he must—
OHATSU: You must have a lot of enemies.
PARIS: I'm not well liked.
OHATSU: I hope I haven't interrupted anything.
PARIS: Nothing I can't finish later.
NARRATOR: The gun has unnerved her, and the way he says—
PARIS: Nothing I can't finish later.
NARRATOR: Unnerves her further. As though he can read her mind he says—

PARIS: I've been cleaning it.

He proves this—the gun comes apart—the black figures take bits of it, proving it is a gun, but not in an operating state. PARIS *grins.*

Not about to give it a head job.

The ghostly attendants assist PARIS *to stick the barrel section in his mouth, by way of demonstration.* OHATSU *takes this image in (Paris the suicide). The barrel shifts and is now held to the side of his head.*

Not about to blow my brains out, if that's your worry.

OHATSU: If blowing your brains out is the name of the game I've got some sake here that's guaranteed to have that effect.

KEIKO displays a bottle of sake that OHATSU *has brought with her. The figures relieve* PARIS *of the pieces of the gun and set them down near the tripod.*

Home alone?

NARRATOR: Yes he nods. But the thought she doesn't want to think keeps returning, the idea she wants to push away keeps coming at her. A minute later, had she arrived and come through the gate (a minute later), come round the house, (a minute later)—what would she have found? Suddenly she staggers forward, like the light perhaps is blinding her, like suddenly her worst fears have been made flesh, like a blood-clot is exploding in her skull.

OHATSU: Argh!

She screams.

NARRATOR: She's become a still point but the world is turning, light but all around her is dark is murder is mayhem, chaos and confusion, hell of a kind.

Lighting and sound effects crash in, marking the start of a thirty second Tarantino-style nightmare. PARIS *falls and lies there, a corpse seeping blood. The walls of the pool are lit in a way that makes them look blood splattered. Like a mat, a scatter of guts and viscera has spread across the floor of the pool. Swift action from the gathered figures produces this image. And the band chimes in with a repeat of an earlier verse.*

SONG: When you can't face the night—but the day has no sun,
          When there's no place to rest—or run,
          When the threat's out there—but also inside,
          Where do you go—or hide?

All freeze except for PARIS, *who gets up.*

PARIS: Are you alright?

NARRATOR: Is it the light, I'm sorry I should turn that off, he says.

PARIS: I'm sorry I should turn that off.

> PARIS *has a remote control unit which he aims towards the house and the shaft of light from the security system dies. A figure snaps the tripod lamp back on. Whatever 'props' and 'items' were used to suggest this vision of Death have vanished as quickly as they came.* PARIS *is talking. It's like* OHATSU *blinked, saw horror, blinked again, and normalcy returned.*

Better?

> OHATSU *composes herself. She notes how the pool scene is as before. The 'invisible' figures and* PARIS *look at her as though nothing 'strange' has happened.*

Not broken?

OHATSU: Me?

PARIS: The sake.

OHATSU: I don't think so.

PARIS: Let us praise the gods for small mercies, a drink at last.

> OHATSU *sees where the sake lies, having been rolled there by the figure who attends her. Its 'travel' had been part of the bent moment we have seen a few moments earlier.*

OHATSU: Actually, a little more light might be nice.

> PARIS *aims the remote. Suddenly the whole pool and surrounds are lit—almost achieving a Californian Hockney-like quality. Night and its shadows snap to day. This catches the shadowy figures in the pool by 'surprise'. They begin to peel off their dark costumes to reveal white clothing underneath in order to blend in better with their surroundings. This shift is marked by a change in the music to the prelude of the song to come.*

PARIS: Ridiculous. An ultra-modern cutting edge state of the art security system guarding what—a near-empty house.

NARRATOR: Absurd.

OHATSU: Was it always that way?

PARIS: Absurd?

OHATSU: Near-empty.

PARIS: No. Crammed with treasure. A burglar's paradise. We'd come home from a weekend in the country and catch them at it—shadowy figures making off with the video and the tape deck, lifting the art works. No lack of chattels. My wife and I tended to use shopping as a substitute for sex.

NARRATOR: She smiles, that's what you did when men made jokes, you smiled.

OHATSU: Also empty.

PARIS: The pool? I'm a bankrupt—I can't afford the chemicals.

OHATSU: But you can afford a gun, and what's that, a ground to air missile launcher?

PARIS: You could say that.

A chorus figure indicates the body of a telescope on the tripod.

OHATSU: A telescope? An astronomer?

NARRATOR: She smiles. It's better to think about the telescope than think about the gun.

PARIS: It's an interest I picked up as a kid—where I lived scanning the heavens was what passed for nightlife. These two prized possessions are about the only booty I beat my wife and the creditors to. I call this my outdoor observatory.

PARIS *has begun adjusting and aligning the telescope.*

I do remember you, you know.

OHATSU: So I've 'come back' to you, have I?

PARIS: It was the baseball team story that did it.

This too is 'weird'. OHATSU, *assisted by the chorus, is jumping in slo-mo off the deck, into the pool. They guide her back up the ladder to repeat the act.* PARIS *is scanning the heavens and doesn't see it happening.*

OHATSU: Go Tigers!

PARIS: The city's baseball team loses—Osaka's in mourning—every young lout worth his salt jumps off the bridge into the—what river was it?

OHATSU: The Dotonbori.

PARIS: I remember you telling me that story—a smile on your lips.

Looking up from the telescope, he turns back and realises OHATSU *is 'in the pool' after her second or third 'jump'. She is coming his way, smiling.*

OHATSU: Same lips.

PARIS: Same smile.

OHATSU: May I?

PARIS: Be my guest.

OHATSU *is keen to use the telescope. She starts staring through the lens piece, scanning the heavens. The Tanabata theme plays as underscore.*

OHATSU: Ever wondered what it would be like to be a star?

PARIS: In what movie?

OHATSU: In the sky.

PARIS: O, in the firmament. Not—me Bogart, you Bacall?

OHATSU: Me Vega, you Althair. Tanabata—have you heard of Tanabata?

PARIS: Isn't it the river that runs into the Dotonbori?

OHATSU: It's a Chinese legend that somehow washed up in Japan. And Vietnam and Kampuchea.

NARRATOR: She tells him the Tanabata story. How—

OHATSU: Vega was a weaver.

PARIS: She wove things.

OHATSU: Cloth. Althair a herder.

PARIS: He herded things.

OHATSU: His flock. The two fell in love but tragically they couldn't marry. When they died.

PARIS: Magically.

OHATSU: They were transformed into stars. A part of the Milky Way. And as it spirals, one night a year the stars are close enough for the two to come together and make love.

PARIS: Which is when you celebrate Tanabata in Japan.

OHATSU: We hang paper lanterns and drape poems about the lovers in the trees.

PARIS: And in China and Vietnam and Kampuchea?

OHATSU: I don't know what they do there.

PARIS: Nice story.

OHATSU: Stories are. It's reality that disappoints.

She has looked away from the lens to PARIS. *And then up.*

It's so quiet, this suburb.

PARIS: Not like Osaka?

NARRATOR: I'm not used to so much—silence, she thinks.

OHATSU: You could hear a pin drop.

PARIS: Or a thought thunk.

NARRATOR: I wouldn't worry, he says, any minute now someone'll rev a motorbike engine, soon a car will pass. Or a window will open and we'll catch a bit of television, courtesy of the neighbours.

PARIS: Hear that?

He bids her listen.

OHATSU: What?

PARIS: Wait. There. Another Christian has just been thrown to the lions.

He explains his joke.

It's the roar of the crowd. Must be a night-game at the WACA. The crowd noise travels across the river. Amplified for some reason, here in the pool, must be the plumbing.

OHATSU: Go Tigers.

PARIS: Eagles, the blue and golds.

In stretching her arm in a barracker's fist, PARIS *has spotted the tell-tale scars of a would-be suicide on* OHATSU's *wrist. A percussive musical chord marks the moment.*

Your arm.

OHATSU: Yes.

PARIS: Scars.

NARRATOR: You ran into a door, he says. One of those ones with razor blades in, she says. And adds how she hates gifted people—the way they get what they do right the first time. You however, he says. I usually make a hash of things, she says.

The musical underscoring and chorus help give a solemn, grave, metaphysical feel to proceedings. It's almost archetypal. Like Adam and Eve meeting. A primal power, something weird, disturbing, is being portrayed, is pulsing below the surface of the realistic remarks they make. It's also shades of Bogart and Hepburn in The African Queen or Streep and Redford or something. We, the audience, know they're in love—or are going to be—but they're acting blase about it—that's the sort of territory we are in.

PARIS: Did that happen because you were a young woman in New York, far from home?

OHATSU: No. It happened at home, and I got sent to New York, the home of—psychotherapy.

PARIS *kisses her scarred wrist.*

PARIS: All better?

OHATSU: All better. In fact I hear music.

PARIS: I wonder whose plumbing that's coming through.

OHATSU: I've run away you see.

PARIS: To join the circus?

OHATSU: I don't know—is this the circus?

PARIS: We've certainly got a big top up top.

OHATSU *is now at the top of the ladder.*

OHATSU: I'm the aerialist.

PARIS: I guess that makes me the clown.

OHATSU: Wheee!

PARIS: We all fall down.

OHATSU *leaps (is carried down) to floor level.* PARIS *does a pratfall with a catcher supporting him and returning him to his feet. Their eyes drink each other in (as it were). They revolve on the spot as though daring each other to make the next move, initiate further physical contact. A major change in the relationship is being marked—from 'old friends have met in the hotel' of Act One—to 'two people are being drawn to each other in a deep way'. A kind of fatal attraction is setting in during Act Two. It triggers a duet.*

SONG: Is this the end of the world as you know it,
         How much pain can you feel and not show it.
         Taken to breaking point here at the frontier of reason,
         Is this bliss your doing—or the work of the gods?
         You cross sanity's border,
         You oughta be scared—but you're not.
         Suddenly against the odds,
         You're swimming—but not in water,
         Swimming—but not in water.
         What bliss.

The music continues. A dance sequence has evolved featuring various carries and lifts that KEIKO *choreographs, seemingly on impulse, and which the rest of this strange white chorus help drive. For* PARIS *and* OHATSU *it's a fantasy, but a joint one—a sexually charged courtship song and dance.*

SONG: Such a reverse of the natural order,
         I feel ancient—and yet newly human,
         All spent—your economy's booming,
         So bent—like you're Alfred E. Newman?
         (No no—madder than *Mad*,
         It's like breathing in a vacuum,
         Slo-mo / go-go / dancing—on a rainbow).
         Suddenly against the odds,
         You're swimming—but not in water,
         Swimming—but not in water.

During the song and dance, the yearning, the longing, the flirting of these lovers is echoed in the movement style of the chorus, led in a quite explicit, even lewd way by KEIKO *and her cohorts. It's slo-mo. Abstracted. This section of the story is foreplay. A part of the overall arc of the piece. Act One was formal, reserved, a first meeting after a long separation. With Act Two—this follow up visit—comes the realisation that they are quite primally attracted to each other. Act Three will hasten towards consummation (and death). Here we're settling into the second stage.* PARIS *makes a formal offer.*

PARIS: Since you've come all this way, I should show you the house, shouldn't I?

OHATSU: Please, I'd like that.

But the music under bids them continue the song.

SONG: How to explain—O what a feeling,
            Insane—your senses are reeling,
            Strange terrain—it's like walking—on the ceiling,
            You oughta be scared but you're not.

Music stops. Silence. Again, PARIS *makes an offer.*

PARIS: Since you've come all this way, I should show you the house.

OHATSU: You already said you would.

PARIS: I did?

OHATSU: You really do have a memory problem, don't you?

PARIS: The house? Ar, yes. It's this way.

He leads her to the ladder. They climb up to the pool deck. Music resumes.

NARRATOR: And he does, he proceeds to show her into his dream home.

The white chorus melt away. KEIKO *and the* NARRATOR *remain.* PARIS *and* OHATSU *step off the deck—it would seem into space. They appear to 'hover', as the music (the Tanabata theme) builds. Meanwhile,* KEIKO *and the* NARRATOR *have climbed from the pool and composed themselves on the deck, following the progress of the lovers away from them towards a giant red disc at the very rear of the stage. Music ends.*

INTERVAL

LOVE TO THE POWER OF HATE

House lights fade and a Japanese folk song about Tanabata is played. Lights come up on the deck. Standing there are the PUPPET PARIS *and the* PUPPET OHATSU. *A musical introduction to the opening song plays under the following dialogue from the puppets. The pool ladder has been removed.*

OHATSU: What are human beings?
PARIS: Filth on two legs.
OHATSU: Are people incapable of great love?
PARIS: Self love perhaps—but only that.
OHATSU: I disagree. I think—

    The live OHATSU *and* PARIS *replace their puppet selves and sing:*

SONG: We are lovers / haters,
            Lovers / traitors—second-raters,
            We are lovers / leavers—born deceivers,
            Lovers and the song of love lives on,
            Lives on where?
            In the bricks in the mortar in the stone of a prison wall?
            No—in the call of a bird in the moaning of a bough,
            In the soughing of a breeze can be heard
            The sigh of some eternal him?
            A cry from some eternal her.
            It's a breath—it's a murmur—it's a song,
            In the stirring of the leaves,
            On the wind as it winds among the trees,
            In the whispering of grass as we pass.
            We are lovers / leavers,
            Lovers / traitors,
            Lovers and the song of love lives on!
            Haters—and that battle's never won!

The lighting changes. The puppets spin back into view as the live OHATSU *and* PARIS *exit at the upper level. Below,* KEIKO *and the* NARRATOR *slide the pool wall open to form a doorway. The trick is that we haven't gone anywhere. We play the pool space as though it is the house. We use music and lighting and acting to sculpt its interior. And scenic magic. For example, we pull drawers out from the pool walls, open cupboard and wardrobe doors. Above, on the pool deck, the two puppet operators (minus their puppets) watch the scene unfolding below. A tour of inspection is underway as* OHATSU *and* PARIS *appear at stage floor level.* KEIKO *and the* NARRATOR *'accompany' them.*

PARIS: Like I said, my wife and the rest of the creditors are fighting over who gets title to the place—meanwhile I caretake the premises. Here, there used to be a big mirror.

OHATSU: But not now.

PARIS: We demolished that in one of our battle royals. And here, even bigger, there was a painting, a Robert Juniper, a Pilbara landscape. I loved it. It reminded me a little of where I come from.

OHATSU: Gone.

PARIS: You can see where it was, the paint has faded unevenly.

NARRATOR: So much space, she says. Tons of it, he says. Storage, she asks.

PARIS: Wall to wall.

OHATSU: May I?

PARIS: By all means.

OHATSU *pulls out a drawer or opens a cupboard door set in a wall.*

OHATSU: Empty.

PARIS: Mmm.

OHATSU *repeats the act with a second door or drawer.*

OHATSU: Also empty. And so little furniture.

PARIS: My wife took whatever she felt entitled to, it happened to be just about everything. In fact no furniture to speak of. I live simply these days.

OHATSU: Like a monk.

PARIS: In a cell.

OHATSU: Next week.

PARIS: Yes. From this cell to another.

> OHATSU *is looking around.* PARIS *has the sake.*

Feel free to wander. I'll see if I can rustle us up some glasses.

OHATSU: Can I be trusted?

PARIS: To do what?

OHATSU: To not steal things.

PARIS: What's to steal?

OHATSU: It was a joke.

PARIS: O yes, jokes, I remember them.

> KEIKO *and the* NARRATOR *'guide'* PARIS *to a rear corner of the pool, stand him there, his back to us 'out' of the action.* OHATSU *continues her exploration.*

NARRATOR: She does as he says. She wanders from room to room. It starts to disturb her—the drawers cupboards empty the wardrobes likewise, no clothes, nothing, in the bathroom just a razor.

> OHATSU *calls out to* PARIS *but needn't because he is returning.*

OHATSU: I'm starting to wonder does anybody even live here.

PARIS: Sorry—no glasses.

OHATSU: We can drink from the bottle.

PARIS: That's what I do.

OHATSU: And eat from the can?

PARIS: No. Can is what I carry.

OHATSU: Mr Fox explained it to us.

PARIS: That was good of him.

OHATSU: How your ex-boss and partner left for Majorca, leaving you to hold the fort.

PARIS: To face the music.

OHATSU: You haven't answered my question: does anybody—

PARIS: Live here? Sure. I do. I eat think weep sleep. Through here's my bedroom. Not a very grown up colour scheme. It was my daughter's room.

NARRATOR: She notices he's hung a sheet across the window. Keeps out the dawn, he says. The dawn can be the cruelest light, she says.

PARIS: That depends how good the night has been.

> *Using foot-holds in the wall, the puppet operators have climbed down to the stage floor. They 'enter' a mattress into proceedings. They unroll it, along with a neat pile of clothes which follow. This setting of objects is almost ceremonial.*

OHATSU: At last, some furniture.

PARIS: Do you class a mattress as furniture? I s'pose you do.

> *Acting younger than her years, trying to wring some joy here, spark up a bit of laughter, chit-chat an end to his contained gloomy vibe,* OHATSU *takes a new tack.*

OHATSU: What thinking?

PARIS: What?

OHATSU: What thinking is a game I used to play with my friend Keiko. I ask you what thinking?

PARIS: And?

OHATSU: You tell me. We think some more. Then you ask me—what thinking?

PARIS: I don't think you'd like to know.

OHATSU: Why?

NARRATOR: But he tells her. Tells her how, not long after he got back from Osaka.

PARIS: Our boy must have been having his afternoon nap in the next room. My wife and I were in here. She'd been showing me the redecorating she'd done while I'd been away and I'd forced her against the wall.

OHATSU: This wall?

PARIS: Yes, and lifted her maternity frock—that's what I'm thinking, thinking how I've always found something sexy about loose clothing. She was pregnant, not too pregnant. I eased her pants down, forced myself upon her.

NARRATOR: You'll wake the boy, she said.

PARIS: But I kept at it.

OHATSU: She wasn't enjoying your attentions.

PARIS: I ploughed on, going down on her.

OHATSU: Going down on her as in licking her cunt?

PARIS: Yes. Going down on her as in licking her cunt.

OHATSU: And feeling her breasts?

PARIS: I was not long, like I said, back from Osaka. And—

NARRATOR: This isn't doing much for you, is it?

PARIS: I said.

NARRATOR: But she didn't answer, wouldn't answer.

PARIS: And there was a moment there.

NARRATOR: When he forced her thighs wider.

PARIS: When I looked up wanting to see her face.

NARRATOR: Only it wasn't her face.

PARIS: It was a Japanese face.

NARRATOR: Was it me? she says. I think so, he says. Oooo, what a wicked thought that is, she smiles.

> *They circle.*

Being in this room reminded me of that, he says. And you?

OHATSU: Me?

PARIS: What are you thinking?

OHATSU: Not 'what are you thinking?' What thinking?

PARIS: Otherwise it's not a game, I s'pose.

OHATSU: That's what Keiko would say. If you don't get it right.

NARRATOR: It's not a game.

> *A pause. A backlighting change as she formulates her thoughts. A moon is glimpsed on a distant cloth.*

OHATSU: This was also not long after we met.

NARRATOR: And she tells him what she's thinking.

OHATSU: I suppose I was drunk, well a little, though that's hardly an excuse.

PARIS: An excuse—sounds interesting already.

OHATSU: It was.

PARIS: An excuse for what?

OHATSU: We were, a group of us, Keiko, some boys from the company, friends. At a moon viewing party, in a park, that's something we do in Japan.

PARIS: View the moon.

OHATSU: And have a party. Think beautiful thoughts is the idea —the beauty of nature, that sort of thing—the clouds caught just so by the moon—that sort of thing—existence being a temporary passing phenomenon—we Japanese, I suppose it's our Buddhist heritage. We were eating, drinking, we'd spread a rug—is picnic that's the word, isn't it?

NARRATOR: Yes, he nods.

OHATSU: Thank you—and I sat down, next to a boy I kind of felt attracted to, nothing special but.

PARIS: I know what you mean.

OHATSU: He was lying there, sake in one hand, the other just somehow palm up. We were in kimono—Keiko and I—that's part of it sometimes.

PARIS: You dress for the occasion.

OHATSU: Yes, and I sat down Japanese style.

> *She has sat this way on the mattress.*

I sat. On his hand. Hard, so he couldn't take his hand away, but pretending I didn't even know it was there. And we kept talking— he to his friends and me to Keiko. And then with my foot.

PARIS: Yes.

OHATSU: Because it was quite near his crotch, with my foot I started to nuzzle, if a foot can nuzzle, into his thigh and along his.

PARIS: Cock.

OHATSU: Yes his cock. And I raised myself slightly, so his hand was free to explore my.

PARIS: Cunt.

OHATSU: Inner thighs, and my bum, which he stroked, in a most pleasant fashion.

PARIS: Good for him.

OHATSU: As he laughed at a joke, as I talked to Keiko, his hand began to find its way past the edge of my pants, all of us chattering gaily, drinking sake, laughing.

PARIS: And of course, viewing the moon.

OHATSU: Of course.

NARRATOR: But in the shadowy world under her kimono there was no moon, just a moist and delicious darkness. And then, when she looked back over her shoulder, perhaps simply to smile encouragement, indicate pleasure—

OHATSU: The same.

PARIS: The same?

OHATSU: As you.

NARRATOR: Instead of your wife you saw a Japanese face—

OHATSU: I saw, not my friend's face but a foreigner's face, your face, and I realised then that's what I'd wanted you to do the night we were alone in the hotel room I'd taken you to, that's what I'm thinking.

PARIS: I see. Sounds somewhat uncomfortable.

OHATSU: It wasn't. Should I show you how we were?

PARIS: I get the picture.

OHATSU: I realised you had entered my dreams and probably would always be there.

PARIS: I didn't enter your dreams.

OHATSU: You did.

PARIS: You entered mine.

OHATSU: Did I?

NARRATOR: Why was he lying—it hadn't been her face—or had it, maybe it had but how could he swear to that now, years later. If she says what thinking again will you tell her the truth—that what you're thinking is you do but also don't remember her—bits of her maybe, the baseball team story, going to that play.

OHATSU: Pardon?

PARIS: Nothing.

NARRATOR: How do you tell someone that memory for you is a problem, that you have too much of it because you've lived too long, done too much, seen too many, evil things, in yourself and in others.

OHATSU: When I told Keiko, that I'd seen your face instead of Keiji's.

PARIS: He's the boy.

OHATSU: Yes, that's when she drew the red heart on your meishi—you were my foreign lover she said. I like this room.

PARIS: Why?

OHATSU: It reminds me of nice things. Of childhood. Of play.

PARIS: A state infinitely preferable to that of being an adult.

OHATSU: Don't you think so?

NARRATOR: He supposed he did.

OHATSU: Here is the pile of clothes—here is the lake—but where are the swimmers?

PARIS: Do you think some accident has happened?

OHATSU: Do you think they've gone swimming late at night and drowned?

PARIS: You might be right, look, here's a note with the clothes.

OHATSU: Ar, that's to cover our tracks.

PARIS: Our tracks? You and me?

> *They exchange a look, gauging each other's attitudes to this fantasy.*

OHATSU: We are escaping.

PARIS: Escaping what exactly?

OHATSU: Our lives of course.

PARIS: Of course, our—lives.

OHATSU: Don't look for us at the nearest McDonald's says the note. That's where we are, having breakfast.

PARIS: Before we mac-flee across the mac-Nullabor going mac-east—I like this line of thought.

OHATSU: Exciting, isn't it?

PARIS: High profile white collar corporate criminal facing nine years jail—

OHATSU: Escapes!

PARIS: This'll be in the papers this'll sell tabloids! The Japanese woman with him—

OHATSU: Escapes too.

> *She smiles, enjoying the pictures they paint. His question introduces a sour note.*

PARIS: And what's she escaping?

OHATSU: A marriage she has agreed to in a moment of weakness and great mental confusion, one more thing in her life she's been too weak to say no to.

> *A pause. Their small talk, their play, has come to an end.*

PARIS: I'm sure the glasses I'm after are in the garage.

> *Backlights and the moon snap out. The side wall of the pool hinges back to allow the main section of the wall to slide open. We will glimpse the Holden through this 'garage door'.*

NARRATOR: He proceeds to show her an Australian institution.

PARIS: This may be new to you, but in Australia you know you've made it if you've got a three car garage.

OHATSU: Even if you haven't got three cars? My, that is a very old car.

PARIS: The Holden? No way. I just stole it last week.

NARRATOR: She laughs, then somehow realises.

PARIS: It's true. Well. Stole's a technicality. The keys were in the boot. Eleven parking tickets on the windscreen, another sixty parking tickets in the glove box. I figured it was a gimme, something the gods had tossed my way.

OHATSU: Aren't you afraid of the police?

PARIS: I'm already facing nine years jail, what's a mere peccadillo like stealing a car amount to?

> *He disappears from view inside the garage.* OHATSU *remains on its threshold.*

NARRATOR: Is it one of those stories?

OHATSU: I still don't believe you.

NARRATOR: You meet in a bar. You tell him your story he tells you his. Later in the carpark you say where are we going? My place he says—how you say—steal a car he says. You spend the next two weeks with this man.

PARIS: Does it matter?

NARRATOR: Then he robs a bank. Commits a murder. Is it one of those stories?

> *Looking for drinking glasses,* PARIS *passes the Holden.*

PARIS: Where Big Red is, I used to park the Audi. I could have afforded better, I just had a soft spot for Audis, men get that way, about cars. Over here's where the wife plonked the Range Rover. Here stood the 1936 Lancia.

OHATSU: A really old car.

PARIS: The Lancia, you bet. That was a restoration job.

> OHATSU *is still looking at the Holden.* PARIS, *accompanied by one of the ghostly attendants, is fossicking amongst objects in the stage left band area.*

The son and I were doing quality time, not that he was old enough to be much help—pass me the head gasket, will you son—I said the head gasket, not the carburettor seal—real quality time it was.

OHATSU: How old is your son?

PARIS: Nine.

OHATSU: Nine years.

PARIS: There it is again, nine years, the magic number.

NARRATOR: He'll be eighteen by the time you get out.

PARIS: It's not worth thinking about.

OHATSU: Sorry?

PARIS: Nothing.

OHATSU: And your daughter?

PARIS: Five going on six.

OHATSU: Six and nine.

PARIS: The dirty number.

OHATSU: Only if you've got a dirty mind. Otherwise: six and nine, ying and yang.

PARIS: Man and woman.

OHATSU: That's my story.

PARIS: And you're sticking to it. Ar, good, the glasses.

> *A chorus figure has handed him two glasses and he is now coming back towards her. The garage door closes. The* NARRATOR *is now at the upper level. The swimming pool ladder is being re-positioned.*

NARRATOR: Suddenly they were back, she wasn't quite sure how, in the swimming pool.

OHATSU: Shall we sit up here?

> *The pool wall has closed across our view of the Holden.* OHATSU *starts to climb the steel ladder to the upper level.*

PARIS: I'll clear these things, if you don't mind. We rarely get a frost here in Perth, but sometimes we do get a dew.

> *He makes towards the gun and the telescope. She is handed the sake and glasses. She sits on the pool edge to watch him.*

OHATSU: The gun and the telescope. In Osaka it was the sword and the chrysanthemum, wasn't it?

PARIS: Was it? What sword was that?

OHATSU: In the play I took you to, the lovers—he killed her then himself.

Behind her, on the deck, the Sonezaki Shinju *lovers enact their slo-mo suicide with a sword. Or, perhaps, the scene in which her obi unwinds. The lovers are played by the* PUPPET OHATSU *and the* PUPPET PARIS, *dressed in the costumes worn by their live counterparts during the earlier insert from the play.*

PARIS: That was the sword. And the chrysanthemum?

OHATSU: Was on my kimono.

PARIS: I liked your kimono.

OHATSU: Silk and steel, the story of Japan. What is it in the west?

PARIS: The gun and the telescope runs it close.

OHATSU: Science.

PARIS: And militarism—isn't that the story of western civilisation?

OHATSU: My, we're getting deep.

PARIS: Add the in-ground swimming pool and we're talking the story of Western Australian civilisation. Amazing, you scrimp, you save, you sweat your guts out to buy 'the dream home'.

OHATSU: It's a lovely home.

PARIS: Is it? You decorate, furnish, renovate, restore. There's the country property as well. Onward. Mush mush. The three cars, you've got them, his, hers and the special project. You landscape the grounds.

OHATSU: Nice.

PARIS: Some fashionable gardener who charges you a thousand bucks to say hello to. You dig the pool, tile it, maintain it, get the outdoor furniture, the barbecue, fully computer operated, you have to read the manual before you can cook a chop—but what have you got, what have you dug for yourself?

He hands bits of the gun, tripod, etc, to the obliging chorus figures.

A fucking grave!

He is in such a state, that he seems to have forgotten his guest, OHATSU, *is there. These are, after all, his last hours. She has been opening the sake. The puppet play insert has run its course and vanished.*

OHATSU: You're funny.

PARIS: Am I?

OHATSU: I have a question, an Audi is?

PARIS: A car.

OHATSU: I thought as much. Cancel the question.

PARIS: Low end of the luxury car market. When I first made the move, from the Commonwealth Bank in Boulder to private enterprise in big bad Perth, an Audi was part of my salary package. Six months into the job I realised I was worth six Audis. I stuck with them. You can see one I pranged from up there.

OHATSU: Really.

PARIS: Sentiment's a strange emotion. I set it up in the back yard. Rigged a drip system. Got an array of ferns, mosses, lichens to grow all over, and in it.

OHATSU: A mossy grotto?

PARIS: The kids called it 'the church'. I'd sit there—the float tank you have when you haven't got a float tank. Were you just passing—or did you come about something specific?

OHATSU: I told you—I've run away.

PARIS: To join the circus.

OHATSU: I think to get away from it. In fact I have a dreadful secret. Come closer and I'll whisper it to you.

> PARIS *approaches. Pauses.*

I have killed mother and father. Closer, there's more.

> *He approaches a step or two. Pauses.*

Sister, brother-in-law, and husband-to-be I've left bound and gagged in a cupboard. A rarely used broom cupboard. On the 23rd floor.

PARIS: Will they be found?

OHATSU: I hope not.

PARIS: And the execrable Foxy-baby?

OHATSU: A nasty piece of work.

PARIS: You can say that again.

OHATSU: No—what I did to him is the nasty bit of work, but for that you'll need to stand here.

> *She is standing on the deck and points to a spot below her. He approaches and stands looking up at her.*

And turn around.

He turns to face front. She holds her sandals, having removed them earlier.

For telling my family such dreadful things about my old and dear friend Mark Paris, the execrable, you'll be pleased to know, has perished.

PARIS: Executed?

OHATSU: Cut from here to here, from ear to ear.

She runs her naked foot across his bare throat.

You like that?

PARIS: I could get used to it.

OHATSU: The news of Foxy-baby's untimely end?

PARIS: That foot across my throat.

OHATSU: Then I'll do it again.

She does so very slowly.

NARRATOR: She tells him how, in Japan, in the pleasure quarter, in the floating world, in the water trade, a woman's naked foot is considered a very erotic object.

PARIS: I can't see why.

He twists to lightly kiss her left foot as she stands above him.

OHATSU: Was that a kiss?

PARIS: A moth, gently landing.

OHATSU: Should I brush it away?

PARIS: It'll only come back.

He repeats the action on her other foot.

OHATSU: Are we moths drawn to the same flame?

PARIS: Or are we the fire itself?

OHATSU: Thought cold. It flares again. All you have to do is stir the embers.

She drops back to a sitting position, wrapping her arms and legs around him. He slowly pushes her legs apart.

PARIS: I should take you.

OHATSU: Take me, I want you to, I think I always have.

PARIS: Back to your hotel.

OHATSU: That I do not want.

The 'Swimming Not In Water' theme is playing under. She slips down the wall into the pool. He is staring off to one side, having walked away.

That I'll resist.

PARIS: I'll overcome you.

OHATSU: You'll overcome me. Let's let the struggle begin.

She is coming towards him.

NARRATOR: Should he tell her the die is cast, that he won't be spending nine years in jail, that these are his last hours, he has entered the country of the last things, his last moon, his last night on earth, his last look at the empty shallow vessel his dream home has become to him, like a ship he sails it, like the last person on the Marie Celeste, moving through it like a ghost.

PARIS: What happened to us in Osaka?

*He has turned and grabbed her hands. There's a savagery, a quality of desperation to both the question and the action. Once more he sees the scars on her wrists. He lets her hands drop. The chorus begins to utter a weird, low pitched, non-verbal chant. Its intensity will rise. They—*KEIKO, *the* NARRATOR, *the two puppeteers—have grouped on the deck level.*

NARRATOR: Still he has barely a clue who she is, or what happened when they met. And yet inside he hears the cells rearranging themselves, as though somewhere deep in his body an inkling, an intelligence, a remembrance of things past is being incubated.

PARIS: Was it love?

OHATSU: I told you—we could have been lovers.

PARIS: But nothing happened so it was love denied?

OHATSU: The worst sort of love.

PARIS: Love hurts.

OHATSU: Love burns.

PARIS: Love makes fools of us.

OHATSU: Fools make love.

PARIS: And we're not fools. Weren't then. Aren't now.

It's like they're locked in some strange dance. OHATSU *kneels.*

OHATSU: Please don't take me back to the hotel.

PARIS: Why?

OHATSU: The police will be there.

PARIS: You're lying.

OHATSU: I'm kneeling, begging.

PARIS: I won't ask you what thinking.

OHATSU: Too frightened to hear what I might say?

PARIS: Too confused to confront what saying it might lead to. If it was love.

NARRATOR: And his body was telling him something, like his skin somehow remembered her.

PARIS: If it was love, why did we deny it?

OHATSU: Things stood in our way.

PARIS: That thing with your foot—that was in the play we saw, right?

OHATSU: Yes.

PARIS: And in your small hotel room you did it again.

OHATSU: I was explaining the play.

PARIS: You drew your foot across my throat.

> *He is behind her kneeling form. He has grasped her hair and drawn his hand across her throat like a knife.*

What you don't know is how hard my heart has become.

OHATSU: I suspect as cold as my own.

> PARIS *gently raises her hair.*

I am a puppet in your hands.

PARIS: Weaving girl.

> *He lets her hair fall.*

OHATSU: Herd boy.

PARIS: Cold nights on a mountain of cash. A life spent herding dollars that in the end made no sense. Perhaps herd boy shouldn't be 'heard' from.

> *He leans towards her ear. She thinks he is about to whisper something, but he bites her instead. She grimaces in pain and her hand shoots to the wound. Again he walks away from her.*

And isn't weaving girl soon to be married?

OHATSU: Woven into the tapestry of someone else's life.

PARIS: Is that a bad thing?

OHATSU: If it means her own life unravels, if what spirit she has left
    dies, can it be good?

PARIS: Good? I was trying to be good. Back then. Is that what stood in
    our way? I was a married man. With a child and a pregnant wife, a
    happy marriage, you were a schoolgirl.

    OHATSU *stands.*

OHATSU: I was nineteen.

PARIS: But a schoolgirl. What is there between men and women?

OHATSU: You tell me.

PARIS: I'll tell you what I hear, I hear a furious chasm.

OHATSU: When lovers reach for each other they bridge that chasm.

PARIS: How long can such a bridge stand?

OHATSU: In our case, until dawn would be nice.

PARIS: How wise would that be?

OHATSU: How unwise the opposite?

PARIS: I should warn you.

OHATSU: I tremble to hear what you'll say.

PARIS: Mine was once the Midas touch, all I turned my hand to—

OHATSU: Turned to gold?

PARIS: Returned a handsome dividend.

OHATSU: And now?

PARIS: The market's depressed.

OHATSU: So bullish—I can't bear to think what you'll do.

PARIS: What are our lives?

OHATSU: What lives in our hearts?

PARIS: What but a ceaseless endless chaos?

OHATSU: Is not the ceaselessness a kind of pattern, the endlessness a
    kind of shape?

PARIS: Fuelled by fear and loathing.

OHATSU: Driven by love.

PARIS: By hate. I'm taking you home.

OHATSU: The long way is not always the wrong way.

PARIS: You haven't heard the message.

OHATSU: Is it in the massage?

PARIS: I destroy whatever's around me.

OHATSU: And if what's around you is already destroyed?

PARIS: I destroy it afresh.

OHATSU: You need the practice.

PARIS: I curdle the very milk of human kindness.

OHATSU: Aren't you saying no such thing exists?

PARIS: Then I curdle whatever ersatz substitute for it there is.

OHATSU: And to think all I hoped for was a last minute fling before I got married, a night on the town.

PARIS: Which town?

OHATSU: Not Albequerque, not Nagoya.

PARIS: A town like Alice? Kalgoorlie.

OHATSU: I thought Paris.

PARIS: You should visit the goldfields while you're here—see where people like me come from.

OHATSU: Paris is a place I've never been, except in my dreams. I thought a last tango.

NARRATOR: The way she says it.

OHATSU: A last tango with Paris.

NARRATOR: Did she realise for him the countdown had begun?

PARIS: Not much of a dancer.

OHATSU: I remember a night club in Osaka.

> *The 'Swimming Not In Water' theme drops out. Silence, for a moment.*

NARRATOR: For the second time a memory of her is surging through his body, a stirring so ancient it seems embedded in every one of his pores, every one of his cells. Had they met in Osaka six years ago and had she slept at the heart of his being ever since? What was it about her? Why this powerful attraction?

PARIS: I'm telling you I don't have time for this.

OHATSU: Is one night too much to ask? Before.

PARIS: Before?

OHATSU: Before I face the music.

PARIS: Get married?

OHATSU: And die all over again.

> *A second verse to the song is sung.*

SONG: Is this the end of the world as you know it,
         One last chance and you don't want to blow it.

Bad scene they're making a movie you don't get the part,
You've shot your final take.
A call—I want you—out of the blue.
And you take new heart,
Washed-up, finished, look how you start,
Swimming—but not in water,
Swimming—but not in water.
What bliss.
Such a reverse of the natural order,
How to explain—O what a feeling,
Insane—your senses are reeling,
Strange terrain—it's like walking—on the ceiling,
Like slo-mo go-go dancing on a rainbow,
Like breathing—in a vacuum.

The music peaks, then changes. Everything changes. PARIS *and* OHATSU *move downstage. This will be the end of the act. The mezzanine begins to revolve.*

PARIS: You're crying.

OHATSU: I'm swimming.

PARIS: But not in water? I don't deserve—

OHATSU: What?

PARIS: Bliss.

OHATSU: What you think is, I can't give it.

PARIS: You think you can?

OHATSU: I don't know what I think—I feel things that's all—that's all I ever do—I feel my way from moment to moment and life seems—

PARIS: Seems?

OHATSU: So long.

PARIS: To me it seems so short.

OHATSU: One more thing we disagree about.

PARIS: Do you drive? If so you can do the driving.

OHATSU: I have an international licence.

The car has been pushed in as the mezzanine turns. OHATSU *and* PARIS *repeat the lovers' duet of disagreement.*

SONG: We are lovers / haters,
           Lovers / traitors—second raters,

We are lovers / leavers—born deceivers,
Lovers and the song of love lives on.

Like an echo, other voices begin to repeat this part of the song. A large cloth is descending to cover the car and mezzanine unit in the shape of a wave that opens the next act. Meanwhile, a huge chorus is singing as it works.

SONG: We are lovers / haters,
Lovers / traitors—second raters,
We are lovers / leavers—born deceivers,
Lovers and the song of love lives on.

The song continues with PARIS *leading,* OHATSU *countering, and a kind of vocal texture coming from the whole company. The car headlights have come on to pick them out before the wave shape enshrouds the vehicle.*

SONG: Lives on where?
In the bricks in the mortar in the stone of a prison wall?
No—in the call of a bird—in the moaning of a bough,
In the soughing of a breeze can be heard
A sigh from some eternal him?
A cry from some eternal her.
It's a breath—it's a murmur—it's a song,
In the stirring of the leaves,
On the wind as it winds among the trees,
In the whispering of grass as we pass.
We are lovers / leavers,
Lovers / traitors,
Lovers and the song of love lives on,
Haters—and that battle's never won.

Lights fade as the music rounds itself off.

END OF ACT TWO

ACT THREE

THE CONSUMMATION IS ALL

The giant cloth will function as a sea cloth (the beach) and trees, foliage (King's Park). A lighting spot is trained on the NARRATOR's face, which comes through this front cloth. The heads of PARIS and OHATSU follow.

NARRATOR: At the hotel Ohatsu refused to leave the car.

PARIS: The answer's no?

OHATSU: Yes—the answer is no! I showed you Osaka.

PARIS: You want me to show you a quokka.

OHATSU: Rottnest Island.

PARIS: Not a problem. I'll phone the yacht club, wake my crew, have the cruiser readied, we'll be there in no time.

OHATSU: You don't really have a boat, do you?

PARIS: Never saw the point—not when my boss had one.

OHATSU: But he's in Majorca.

NARRATOR: She had read all the brochures.

PARIS: You like the idea of swimming naked?

OHATSU: Are you averse to that? Or do you think Australians are the only people in the world who know how to body surf?

> *The heads of PARIS and OHATSU disappear. The front cloth becomes like a water cloth, night lighting on an ocean swell. The scene continues as though they're treading water. Her head has appeared. Then his. There is a carefree happy-go-lucky feel to all this, a delirium of sorts. This is what the music is telling us.*

NARRATOR: They settled for Swanbourne, where they trod water and drank in the stars. Said things like.

OHATSU: I'm in recovery.

PARIS: From?

OHATSU: Life.

NARRATOR: Said things like.

PARIS: Are you going to make it?

OHATSU: Why don't I let you know a year from now?

NARRATOR: Said things like.

PARIS: I wonder what the poor people are doing.

OHATSU: Starving, as usual.

PARIS: I should know, being poor myself.

OHATSU: Are you starving?

PARIS: This body surfing—

OHATSU: Gives you an appetite.

> *The heads of the lovers disappear again and the sea cloth lighting changes to another colour.*

NARRATOR: After Swanbourne it was Northbridge. A Vietnamese takeaway he knew. After that they drove back across the railway bridge and along Hay Street.

PARIS: Hey!

OHATSU: Don't you like my driving?

PARIS: Pass.

> *The heads have appeared again.*

NARRATOR: They'd struck a bargain. She'd pay for the meal—but he'd choose the place they went to eat it.

OHATSU: Here?

PARIS: Reverse a little.

> *Their heads having thrust further forward, disappear once more. So does the NARRATOR's face. The fabric is parted from either side by the NARRATOR and KEIKO to reveal the car roof where PARIS and OHATSU now stand.*

Is this love?

OHATSU: Is this love?

PARIS: Lust?

OHATSU: Lust?

PARIS: Or plain madness?

OHATSU: Or plain madness?

PARIS: And six years ago what was it?

OHATSU: And six years ago what was it?

PARIS: We said no to it then.

OHATSU: We said no to it then.

PARIS: What are we saying to it now?

OHATSU: What *are* we saying to it now?

PARIS: Will you stop repeating what I'm saying?

OHATSU: Will you stop repeating what I'm saying?

PARIS: Bitch.

OHATSU: Bitch.

PARIS: It isn't hard to see how people can get so fucked in the head.

OHATSU: It isn't hard to see how people can get—that I do know something about—like I told you, I'm in recovery.

PARIS: Me—I fear I'm in decline.

> *They sit on the car roof. The continued exertions of* KEIKO *and the* NARRATOR *arranging the fabric landscape around the car, bring into view the* PUPPET OHATSU *and the* PUPPET PARIS, *seated on the bonnet of the car.*

So, what do you think?

OHATSU: I like it.

PARIS: Our very own King's Park rooftop restaurant!

> *The puppets have the food,* PARIS *and* OHATSU *have the sake. They toast each other.*

OHATSU: To us.

PARIS: To Dotonbori—Osaka.

OHATSU: Perth—King's Park.

PARIS: Kampei.

OHATSU: Kampei.

NARRATOR: They ate they drank they considered their situation.

> *They drink and look around. The puppets are using chopsticks to dine on various delicacies. Delicacy of operation—the wiping of a mouth with a serviette, etc, is very much a feature of the puppetry in this sequence. The overall image is as if* PARIS *and* OHATSU *are drinking in one dimension, shadowed by a version of themselves eating in another. Sometimes it is a mirror effect, more often it deepens and extends the visual image as a whole. There's a unifying moment when a distant police or ambulance siren draws the focus of all four. Then the eating and drinking resumes.*

They ate they drank they shifted their attention to the big questions.

OHATSU: Is there a life after death?

> *The complexity of this picture is augmented by the presence of* KEIKO *and the* NARRATOR *looking on. The musicians also have the lovers under surveillance, adding a sparse musical underscore to proceedings.*

For that matter is there a death after life? It's the same question put in a slightly different way.

PARIS: You're talking another world, outside, beyond this one?

OHATSU: A parallel universe for example.

PARIS: Mmm.

OHATSU: A world that dogs, that shadows our own, a mirror reverse say, of our world. Ours, it's generally agreed, is a material world.

PARIS: I can't argue with that—I drink therefore I am.

OHATSU: The other would be an anti-material world, a parallel universe that thrust matter from it. What's coming into being here is going out of existence there—what goes out of existence as matter here becomes, in that parallel world, spirit. There, matter is drained away—here, it accumulates. There, the spiritual is all—here, the spirit is constantly eradicated, wound down to nothing. Keiko argued such a relationship between worlds was possible, even probable given—

PARIS: Given what?

OHATSU: The way human beings are, there would have to be an alternative for the universe to make any sense.

PARIS: And you? Do you think as she did?

OHATSU: I think of this world as the only one there is.

PARIS: But is it? Lately.

NARRATOR: If he'd had a beard, he would have stroked it.

OHATSU: You should have a beard.

PARIS: What—why?

OHATSU: You could stroke it in a learned fashion.

PARIS: Lately.

OHATSU: Stroke stroke.

PARIS: I've been thinking about the way we cast a shadow—or we see a reflection of ourselves in a mirror—or we glimpse something moving in a shop window and we're convinced, if only for a split second, that it's someone else.

OHATSU: But it's us trapped in glass.

PARIS: Yes but we know, via reflections, that we repeat ourselves here and there throughout this world—what if we repeat ourselves in other worlds? Do you see what I'm saying?

OHATSU: I see what you're saying.

PARIS: I'm saying—I think I'm saying—that when I walk beside a lake and I see myself reflected there.

OHATSU: Ourselves reflected there, we're hand in hand walking round a lake.

PARIS: Is that us?

OHATSU: An extension of us, yes.

PARIS: Or could it be, not us, but creatures like us, trying to be us, trapped, held, reaching towards us from another, maybe the next, world?

OHATSU: The evidence for this other, this next world being?

PARIS: At the moment? And in our world? Only what I say, reflections in the glass, the mirror, the lake. But what if they're like a door— they're a door we lack the key for, until some moment like—

OHATSU: Death?

PARIS: Like death—when you fall into your own image and in doing that slip beyond this world into a new dimension. I sound like a hippy?

OHATSU: Either that or Einstein.

PARIS: And what if at that moment, in that instant, you experience not closure.

OHATSU: Not closure.

PARIS: But an opening.

OHATSU: An opening.

PARIS: A sort of fracture occurs, a slippage between worlds. What if you see there your self in all manner of worlds stretching forward and back, extending outward downward upward inward. On view, perhaps for only a whisker, a milli-second, is any and every you that's ever been or will be in any and every place position location condition you'll ever be or have ever been at or in.

OHATSU: Are you making this up or does someone write your scripts?

PARIS: You sense that every kink and twist in cosmic time spawns a new and yet ancient you. We are both one, but also ten thousand ten million ten trillion selves.

OHATSU: The self, endlessly repeats itself?

PARIS: In this world and in all possible worlds.

OHATSU: That is all there is and we keep dancing.

PARIS: We are spread, or we spread ourselves, like a pack of playing cards, through all space and all time.

OHATSU: And in this pack of cards spread throughout space and time, we are only always one card. You're always—

PARIS: The Jack of Spades.

OHATSU: And I'm the Queen of Hearts for now, forever—

PARIS: And for us there is only that—the same theme, infinitely varied but endlessly re-occurring. Six years ago.

OHATSU: The Jack met the Queen.

PARIS: Tonight.

OHATSU: Jack meets Queen again. And after tonight?

PARIS: Some time hence like an echo of an echo of an echo we'll meet all over again, play out the same love affair—what if that's our karma?

OHATSU: Like Vega and Althair? In fact the Tanabata you have when you're not having the real Vega and Althair.

PARIS: We could be the real Vega and Althair.

OHATSU: Different idea, same cosmic territory. They fall to earth every year for one night.

PARIS: And this year?

OHATSU: Us, ours are the bodies they snatch, we are the chosen two. You're pretty deep for a businessman.

PARIS: Do you think the business of the world is conducted by idiots?

> OHATSU *slides from the roof of the car to gather the take-away things, taking chopsticks from the puppets, etc, placing containers back in their plastic bags. The sound of a magpie carolling.*

OHATSU: I know what I think—I am because I eat. We've had the main course—what else is on the menu?

PARIS: I thought something sweet—moist—sticky.

OHATSU: Sex—I like this 'Paris by night' tour of Perth.

PARIS: It starts with a walk.

OHATSU: A chance to stretch our legs.

PARIS: For dessert.

OHATSU: We deserve it.

PARIS: What the French call—

OHATSU: Dying the little death—in the bushes up against a tree? What bird—

PARIS: Is that? A magpie.

OHATSU: *Nani*. [Rubbish.]

PARIS: An Australian magpie.

OHATSU: O. Are they different to Japanese ones?

PARIS: Are yours black and white?

OHATSU: Just black.

PARIS: Ours are two toned.

OHATSU: Will I see one?

PARIS: Pretty hard not to, except at night. Not even dawn—but that's how they are, magpies. Weird. It can be one in the morning.

OHATSU: It's going on three.

> *She has taken the rubbish to the band area to dump.*

PARIS: If there's a moon up they'll give it a song.

OHATSU: But there is no moon.

PARIS: Then the city lights have got it fooled.

> *They listen as the magpie's song continues. A response from another magpie is heard.*

OHATSU: Two of them—are they lovers?

PARIS: They could be enemies.

> *He, too, slips to the ground from the roof of the car, carrying the sake.*

There's an aboriginal story about magpies. How once all the creatures of the earth lived in darkness.

OHATSU: Not like our enlightened times.

PARIS: And a giant canopy hung over the world, pressing down, and every known beast, insect, bird, be it fish or fowl, lived close to the ground, their heads bowed. Then one day, whilst eating, a certain magpie lifted its head and its beak pierced the canopy.

OHATSU: Light flooded in.

PARIS: Splashing that magpie. And to this day magpies have been.

OHATSU: Black and white.

> *The ghost of* KEIKO *and the* NARRATOR *are preparing to reposition the fabric landscape.*

PARIS: And so surprised was it by this event that it let out a call, and that's—

OHATSU: The call of the magpie.

PARIS: Still heard at dawn, as each new day continues to catch the magpie by surprise. A little something I learnt at school in Kalgoorlie. It's my revenge.

OHATSU: For?

PARIS: Your Tanabata story.

OHATSU: There are magpies in the Tanabata story.

PARIS: Really?

OHATSU: Japanese—well no—celestial magpies. They're mentioned in the puppet play I took you to—a passage they made us learn at school. But I'll spare you the details.

> OHATSU *and* PARIS *exit. To shamisen underscore, the ghost of* KEIKO *dances. The* NARRATOR *quotes a Chikamatsu passage, in Japanese, about how one year when the Milky Way is in flood and it looks like the stars, Althair and Vega, won't be able to join each other. Magpies come to their aid and build a bridge of twigs, allowing the star-crossed lovers to meet. The lighting reverts to watery effects. The fabric begins to rise and get hung over the scene like a canopy. The* PUPPET OHATSU *and the* PUPPET PARIS *are positioned on the hood of the car to look like airline passengers. As the car is pushed to one side, the musicians sing.*

SONG: You've drunk and you've eaten,
        You're feeling fed,
        The hostess with a smile comes down the aisle,
        Saying she knows where there's a bed.
        But something is not quite being said.
        In need of correction—wrong direction,
        Your plane is losing height,
        This could be your final flight,

The horror the terror—computer error.
The blip that's you on the radar screen
Is fast dropping out of sight.
Going going gone you're on
A blind date with a crash site.
In need of correction—wrong direction,
Your plane is losing height,
This could be your final flight,
The horror the terror—computer error.

Blackout the puppet passengers. The lighting reverts to landscaping effects. A flickering fluoro in the lower part of the mezzanine unit picks out OHATSU *and* PARIS.

OHATSU: What is this place?

PARIS: An information area, with displays, a map of the park, an old annual report.

OHATSU: Do we read it?

PARIS: I don't—I've read it before—but you can.

OHATSU: I can try, it's not easy.

PARIS: Why, because I've cupped your breast and I'm flicking your nipple.

OHATSU: That's part of the problem, but the fluorescent light—

PARIS: Is on the blink.

OHATSU: Keiko would do that. Remove my bra without me even seeming to notice.

PARIS: When you played what thinking?

He lets her bra fall to the ground.

OHATSU: Or when I was reading, sneak up on me from behind.

PARIS: You and Keiko had a lesbian affair?

OHATSU: We were young women discovering our sexuality.

PARIS: She?

OHATSU: Discovered hers.

PARIS: You?

OHATSU: I found it an interesting journey. It says here there's an underground orchid.

PARIS: Yes. But not in King's Park.

OHATSU: No. It's found only in one part of Western Australia.

PARIS: A small area—in the centre.

OHATSU: A form of flora unique to this state.

> *The* NARRATOR *has entered, holding an empty frame. She stands there as part of the display* OHATSU *is reading. The lovers sing.*

SONG: Have you ever thought of making love and dying,
    Have I ever thought of making love and dying?
    Have you ever thought how shocking (wicked),
    Joyous (wild),
    How out there that could be?
    You got a ticket for the last train,
    Somebody's saying—somebody's saying,
    I'm glad you're catching it with me.

> *They kiss. Then* OHATSU *screams.* PARIS *looks alarmed.*

PARIS: Is it the light?

OHATSU: It's Keiko, she's hanging there.

NARRATOR: He takes a rock. He hurls it thinking to smash the light. Instead the fluoro comes on and stays on.

PARIS: See. Nothing. No-one.

> *But the ghost of* KEIKO *is hanging by a rope, off to one side.*

NARRATOR: When he asks she tells him.

PARIS: This thing with you and Keiko.

OHATSU: Can we go somewhere else?

NARRATOR: It's a Cinderella story. How she's left there, holding two shoes. Keiko's shoes.

> PARIS *and* OHATSU *have gone elsewhere. The* NARRATOR *picks up the discarded bra.* KEIKO *unknots the rope and ties it around her own waist. She 'dances' an enactment of the following story.*

Keiko's been hit by a car, stepping from the pavement, outside a club, hit, and the impact carries her a hundred yards down the street, lifts her from the shoes she's wearing, carries her a hundred yards. That's how far before she finally slides away from the car's bodywork.

> *The ghost of* KEIKO *slumps, then rewinds to repeat the action.*

Ohatsu tells him how she picks up the shoes left there on the road (it's a Cinderella story) and runs down the street chasing the car and finds Keiko's crushed body hurled against a tree guard, explains how the face is unmarked, just a string of blood—of the intensest red—coming from her mouth down her chin drip drip dripping onto her blouse.

> PARIS *and* OHATSU *are seated in one of the band areas. She is drinking from the bottle. Her own shoes are set to one side.*

PARIS: You saw all that happen?

OHATSU: I'm left there holding the shoes. And I saw more than the car—I saw who was driving it.

NARRATOR: But of course she didn't really know what she was saying.

OHATSU: I was mad with grief, out of my mind.

NARRATOR: The son of such an important man would never drive so recklessly, and if he had would certainly stop after such an accident.

OHATSU: The police said it couldn't have been the person I saw.

NARRATOR: That he was in Nigata that night. That he had witnesses to prove it. That his car had been stolen.

PARIS: And you got sent to New York?

OHATSU: New York.

PARIS: To undergo psychiatric rehabilitation.

OHATSU: I was mad—mad to think justice would be done.

PARIS: Did they find the car?

OHATSU: Two years ago.

PARIS: In Nigata?

OHATSU: In Osaka. At the bottom of the harbour.

PARIS: The bottom of the harbour, eh?

NARRATOR: They are by a water tank, a concrete water tank.

> *They sing.*

SONG: Have you ever thought of making love while drowning,
         You wave but people on the beach think you're clowning round.
         You're a snowball—on a quick trip to hell,
         A dipstick a dropkick with a chopstick a toothpick,
         A matchstick's chance
         Of riding out the swell.

Like you're Chicken Little's wishbone thrown
At a raging sea.
You decide to face the music.
Nearby somebody is saying
It sounds like the last waltz to me.
I'd be honoured—ever so honoured,
If you'd dance the last waltz with me.

They kiss. The NARRATOR *and* KEIKO *focus them.*

NARRATOR: If only we'd found them that way by the tank.
PARIS: What game are we playing now?
OHATSU: Drop the sake.

She hands PARIS *the bottle.*

PARIS: I drink.
OHATSU: And I empty—your pockets—just checking for sharp objects.

As she removes his belt with one hand, her other hand goes into his pocket.

NARRATOR: That would be nice would it not—frozen there against the concrete, like lovers on a Grecian urn, a belt left on the ground, a hint of love-making in the air like an aura around them.
PARIS: Fuck me!
NARRATOR: But it wasn't to be. The sprinkler system started up, three a.m., on the dot, and on them.
OHATSU: What'll we do?

KEIKO *is training a sprinkler head their way. The percussive sound of the sprinkler is a preface to the song.*

SONG: You make the most of the moment the question's why,
The answer's always: why not?
You make the most of the moment is this all there is,
It feels like all that we've got.
Maybe if the earth moves a little,
It proves that a little means a lot.
A miss is a miss is a miss is a miss,
But a lover's kiss
Always hits the spot.

NARRATOR: Had they frozen there, wet and laughing, melted there, in time into that wall, in time a red stain from the artesian water would form on her legs and on his bare arm caught moving up her calf from her ankle to her knee, would that not be a beautiful picture, a snapshot to treasure for all time?

As though frozen, OHATSU *and* PARIS *are 'framed' by the* NARRATOR, *who still carries the display area frame. The lovers depart for another area. The* NARRATOR *picks up the belt, and* KEIKO *the shoes left behind.*

Alas, when next we find them—we find them in a darker place.

PARIS: You can see here how there's been a fire.

OHATSU: Very interesting for a Japanese tourist.

PARIS: These we call blackboys, but after the fire they're—

OHATSU: Even blacker?

PARIS: And the banksias—

OHATSU: Blacker still—but the white boy—what of him?

PARIS: He is not a happy boy.

OHATSU: Why?

PARIS: Your story has angered him—your story has reminded him of how wicked the world is.

OHATSU: Is he wicked?

PARIS: He is very wicked, ask anyone in Perth.

OHATSU: And am I wicked?

PARIS: You are a weak willed slut—and must be taught a lesson.

He has bound OHATSU *with his jacket. As the* NARRATOR *and* KEIKO *hand him the bra and belt, he binds her further.*

OHATSU: I must be tied up with my own clothing.

PARIS: Yes.

NARRATOR: And some of his.

OHATSU: And some of his.

PARIS: Yes.

OHATSU: Because I wasn't strong enough to fight them—because I let them overcome me—because I was unable to take vengeance in Keiko's name—I must be punished.

PARIS slaps her.

And you like punishment.

PARIS: Maybe for me punishment is all that is left.

The bound OHATSU *is tied to a tree branch which* KEIKO *holds.*

SONG: Have you ever thought of making love in a ring of fire,
Waking up in a hot-bed licked by fingers of flame?
In a last embrace you take your lover,
A frieze of passion you seize what seconds remain,
On the morrow combing the ashes, after the inferno,
We hear forensic explain
That these two lovers came,
They took their pleasure,
Even as they went—in pain.

Then PARIS *leaves. Eyes closed,* OHATSU *waits to be kissed. It's* KEIKO *who kisses her as the musicians and the* NARRATOR *sing.*

SONG: You make the most of the moment the question's why,
The answer's always: why not?
You make the most of the moment is this all there is,
It feels like all we've got.
Maybe—if the earth moves a little,
It proves that a little means a lot.
A miss is a miss is a miss is a miss,
But a lover's kiss
Always hits the spot.

Stirring, as in a swoon, OHATSU *looks around.*

OHATSU: Where is he, is he out there watching, waiting?

NARRATOR: Possibly.

OHATSU: He'll step from the darkness to have his way with me.

NARRATOR: Possibly.

OHATSU: He knows I'm bound.

NARRATOR: Head to toe.

OHATSU: I can't stop him doing whatever he pleases.

NARRATOR: Even if you wanted to you couldn't.

OHATSU: I couldn't say no to his cock in my mouth.

NARRATOR: In your cunt, between your breasts.

OHATSU: I'd have to accept it.

NARRATOR: You're prevented from saying no, you're powerless, weak, the strength has been drained from you.

OHATSU: He's not there, is he?

NARRATOR: Possibly not.

OHATSU: He doesn't want me, won't take me, not even back to the hotel?

NARRATOR: No.

OHATSU: Argh!

NARRATOR: She has heard in the distance a car start up and tears herself free of her bonds. She runs. Staggers. Seeks which way but can't tell where the sound is coming from. Is it the car they came in? She's sure it is but blackboys and the branches of low growing banksias tear at her flesh—rip her clothes more even than he has—fallen logs trip her up.

> *She falls, twists, tries to free herself, crawls, staggers through the fabric landscape with the NARRATOR and KEIKO following. The sound of a car engine idling. The puppet operators emerge from under the fabric, tearing it away to reveal the car. OHATSU, like PARIS, is no longer in view. A light comes up on the car as the PUPPET OHATSU enters from her nightmarish 'journey'. She approaches the passenger side and opens the door.*

But Paris is not inside the car, just the smell of—

> *She pulls back as gas spills from the car's interior. The PUPPET OHATSU looks around. The PUPPET PARIS is to one side looking on. He steps towards and opens the driver's door. Cuts the engine. They look at each other across the hood. She walks around her side of the car.*

She sees now what he's done. He has run a length of plastic hose from the muffler back into the car. Sees now what he has in mind. Just testing the set-up, he says.

> *The PUPPET PARIS sets her mobile phone down on the hood.*

I borrowed your mobile he says. Rang the wife. Thinking she might let me speak to the kids. And? asks Ohatsu. She wouldn't have a bar of it, he says. Poor Mark. Poor me. Poor us.

> *The puppets stare at each other. As they embrace, OHATSU and*

PARIS *enter at mezzanine level and also embrace. A song is heard.*

SONG: And maybe if the earth moves a little,
It proves that a little means a lot.
A miss is a miss is a miss is a miss,
But a lover's kiss
Always hits the spot.

The lovers, PARIS *and* OHATSU, *look down on their puppet selves and narrate.*

PARIS: What thinking?

OHATSU: But it's as though she hasn't heard.

PARIS: I said what thinking?

OHATSU: And yet she has heard, and is thinking. Of a life stretching before her as empty of meaning as it is long, of a marriage she's agreed to against her will, and of the weakness of her will. How bankrupt she feels.

PARIS: Is what thinking a game you don't feel like playing any longer?

OHATSU: Are you as sick of games as I am, she says.

They sing a new verse of this mini-opera, during which, mystically, the car doors open. The NARRATOR *and* KEIKO *leave, their night's work done. The* PUPPET OHATSU *and* PUPPET PARIS *are placed in the car, bound for death's wonderland. The engine starts, the doors close and the puppet operators depart.*

SONG: It's like your clothes are stitched by bullets,
The hull of your boat's been holed,
You thought as a kid will I ever grow up.
Now you know you'll never grow old,
Fortune favours the brave they say,
But the brave if they are to carry the day,
Have to be there when the dice is rolled.
Fortune favours the brave they say,
Who dares wins but they who dare
Have to care if they're to be bold.

PARIS *and* OHATSU *sing to each other about what it's like for them in the car, their last seconds of life, as it were.*

SONG: Have you ever thought of making love after a crash?
          The windscreen's smashed the front end's gone,
          It's gore not four on the floor,
          More gore than you saw
          In that movie *Mash*.

          This crash / not flash / feels final / acid's eating vinyl,
          Do you still want me / course I do / where are you?
          Done my dash on the dash.
          What say I turn a little squirm a bit I'll
          Be able to stroke your thigh.
          What say you if I—unzip your fly?
          We're making love and love can't die.

          I'll suck your tit,
          I'll grip your cock,
          I'll lick your clit,
          I'll jack you off.
          Does the pain—it doesn't hurt me.
          Should I—keep talking dirty.
          If I could I would go down on you,
          If you could I would want you to.
          Is that the fire brigade?
          Could be cops—could be an ambulance.
          What chance us getting laid-out,
          Getting laid!

          The music continues as the lights fade on the lovers singing.

SONG: I'm glad you're lying here with me,
          I'm glad you're dying here with me,
          I'm glad you're lying here with me.

          They've retreated. In the silence, two figures, MINH *and* GAVIN, *appear. The light of early morning picks them out. They recount their roles in this drama.*

GAVIN: I work near here—the insurance company I work for has its building near here—I sometimes jog here before I start work.

MINH: I saw him by the car—the hotel's not far—I'd worked a double shift and sometimes I go home through King's Park—that's what I was doing—he was first here, I was second.

GAVIN: I saw the car—I looked in—I saw her—then I saw him—I saw the mobile on the hood and started ringing triple O.

MINH: I saw him by the car—he called out to me—said there was an emergency—I looked in—and saw Mark Paris—and her. She's a guest at the hotel I said, the hotel I work at I said.

GAVIN: We waited there—for the police, the tow truck, the ambulance—the forensic team—they arrived—a crowd gathered.

MINH: A crowd, and the people in charge, they ran a stay back ribbon round the site.

GAVIN: But before that—

The ghost of KEIKO *has entered. She cordons off the site with a ribbon streaming from her back. On the upper level, a puppet operator has begun to create a tableau using a toy ambulance, police car, tow truck, etc, like a kid at play in a sandpit. The Tanabata theme provides a musical underscore to this whole sequence.*

MINH: Before all that happened we saw what we saw.

GAVIN: Later I found out she saw what I saw.

MINH: We saw the same vision.

GAVIN: Only later did we dare to talk about it.

MINH: And then only to ourselves.

The operators and KEIKO *make for the car.*

GAVIN: The car opening up.

MINH: In sections, in two halves.

GAVIN: Half was a mossy place, green.

MINH: He lay there. The half where she lay, that was bamboo.

GAVIN: Cherry trees maybe.

MINH: Paper lanterns, paper decorations, paper streamers, hanging there in the trees.

GAVIN: Like a street scene.

MINH: In miniature.

GAVIN: Bonsai maybe.

MINH: A Tanabata Festival street scene.

GAVIN: Two stars, hanging.

Sections of the car have hinged open. Inside we see OHATSU *and* PARIS *as if on funeral biers.* OHATSU *is in a small setting of bamboo and paper lanterns like a postcard from a Tanabata festival.* PARIS *is laid out in a mossy grotto like the one mentioned when he spoke of his pranged Audi. We hear a magpie as the dawn light breaks.*

MINH: We heard the same music.

GAVIN: But didn't want to say it at the time.

MINH: Said it later—couldn't believe it at the time.

GAVIN: During counselling it came out.

MINH: It's not easy. To find something like that is bad enough but when something truly weird happens—

GAVIN: You think—

MINH: I'm mad.

GAVIN: How can this be?

MINH: When you've been working long hours your head isn't always clear, your thinking isn't always—

GAVIN: Straight.

MINH: That's right. You think you're seeing things—

GAVIN: I knew him, you see.

MINH: Hearing things.

GAVIN: He as good as killed my parents. I didn't know whether to volunteer that to the police or not—about knowing him—about hating him—about having wished him dead.

MINH: You don't know what to say. I felt strange cos she came from my hotel. How will this look I was thinking.

GAVIN: Things get twisted.

MINH: I didn't want trouble.

GAVIN: We met again at counselling.

MINH: And once more later.

GAVIN: To talk it through, between ourselves.

MINH: To talk it over—seeing her.

GAVIN: Seeing the car open up.

MINH: Seeing her walk away towards someone else.

GAVIN: A woman.

MINH: Saying.

OHATSU: Keiko is that you?

GAVIN: And in the trees turning to look—

MINH: And smiling.

GAVIN: There's this other woman, dancing, in King's Park.

MINH: And seeing him rise up.

GAVIN: As from a grave.

MINH: And come towards you.

GAVIN: It was me he came towards.

MINH: Saying—

GAVIN: 'Say it'.

MINH: Saying: 'Say it, Gavin, say it'.

GAVIN: Say what?

MINH: You said 'say what', I heard you say that.

GAVIN: 'What you always say.'

MINH: Mark Paris was talking to you.

GAVIN: And I say: why don't you die?

MINH: And he says, he said.

PARIS: What if Gavin—what if I'm trying to.

> *The car is slowly closing up again.*

What if Gavin—I'm trying to but—think about it Gavin—I'm trying to end it—but I can't! It doesn't end.

MINH: They were in the car—but they stepped out of the car.

GAVIN: It didn't make sense. They were corpses in the car.

MINH: But out of the car.

GAVIN: I put it from my mind.

MINH: I made myself focus other things.

> OHATSU *and* KEIKO *are moving away from the miniature tableau on the upper level.* PARIS *is climbing to reach it, pausing briefly to look at the child's toys.*

GAVIN: And I saw the tow truck guy talking to the cops.

MINH: And you thought.

GAVIN: I thought something shocking.

MINH: You thought it's top to bottom.

GAVIN: It's all over, it's everywhere, it's top to bottom.

MINH: The towies and the cops.

> *The operator has resumed his child's play on the upper level, introducing doll-sized figures.*

GAVIN: Thick as thieves I thought—I thought it's taking some pens home from the office—it's using the stationery—it's putting your letters in with the company mail-out—it's as small as that—it's as big as buying and selling the world—it's corrupt all over— bottom to top.

MINH: I just thought—I saw them put the sheet over Mark Paris—I thought funny people—Australians—the way they do business.

GAVIN: You thought funny people?

MINH: I thought maybe he sees it now, but too late—I thought Mark Paris, Alan Bond, Christopher Skase, those snakes—do they think what they do won't rebound on them—do they think they can get away with it—that it won't come back at them—and if not them—then it'll be their children who'll suffer—or their children's children—they don't think forward, they don't think back, they only think now, me me me.

GAVIN: What's in their heads, you thought that?

MINH: In Vietnam we do business we don't just think this deal is for today—it's not just for today—or next week or next year—it's for a hundred years—you think about that—how it'll be for your family a hundred, a thousand years from now. And you feel, too, your ancestors looking at you—those who come before you—those who come after. You think yesterday, you think tomorrow—you try to think seven generations ahead, seven generations behind not just—I don't understand.

GAVIN: Funny people you reckon, Australians.

The music for a final song has begun under.

SONG: You gotta hit quit, a story,
             Let it sit, a story,
             Let it lie let it die,
             Have your say walk away,
             A final twist but that's your gist,
             That's it, your story.
             Have a laugh have a cry,
             Cross a tee dot an i,
             Bend it—but end it.

GAVIN: Maybe they're from some other planet, these people, these stars of Australian finance.

MINH: Do you believe that?

GAVIN: No.

MINH: Nor do I—but what goes down comes around—that I do believe.

They exit.

SONG: Let it lie let it die a story,
          You gotta let it go, a story,
          Tie the bow.
          Have your say walk away,
          Then go—call it quits.
          It's—
          Just a story.

The lights have closed down to just the koto being played. The ghost of KEIKO *comes forward to look over the musician's shoulder. Everyone else has gone.*

END OF PLAY